THINKING OUTSIDE THE PRIZE BOX

NAVIGATING **CHALLENGING BEHAVIORS** IN TODAY'S CLASSROOM

COPYRIGHT

Published by Gryphon House, Inc.
P. O. Box 10, Lewisville, NC 27023
800.638.0928; 877.638.7576 [fax]

Visit us on the web at
www.gryphonhouse.com.

Library of Congress Control Number:
2024952716

BULK PURCHASE

Gryphon House books are available for special premiums and sales promotions as well as for fund-raising use. Special editions or book excerpts can also be created to specifications. For details, call 800.638.0928.

DISCLAIMER

Gryphon House, Inc., cannot be held responsible for damage, mishap, or injury incurred during the use of or because of activities in this book. Appropriate and reasonable caution and adult supervision of children involved in activities and corresponding to the age and capability of each child involved are recommended at all times. Do not leave children unattended at any time. Observe safety and caution at all times.

TABLE OF CONTENTS

INTRODUCTION

Eating an egg a day as a part of a healthy diet for healthy individuals is a reasonable thing to do.

—JO ANN CARSON, PROFESSOR OF CLINICAL NUTRITION
(*AMERICAN HEART ASSOCIATION NEWS*, 2018)

Egg yolk and red meat should be avoided . . . to prevent cardiovascular disease and stroke.

—DAVID SPENCE AND COLLEAGUES
(*THE JOURNAL OF THE AMERICAN HEART ASSOCIATION*, 2021)

When I was a child, no one spent too much time thinking about eggs. People ate what they ate, and that was that. But I remember a time when things began to change. Damning new evidence had appeared, suggesting that eggs were, in fact, killing us all. In a sick form of revenge for stealing their unfertilized cloaca fruits,* chickens were clogging our arteries with cholesterol, leading to heart attacks every year for millions of Americans. We had domesticated these dinosaur descendants, eating their wings as Super Bowl snacks. But chickens were playing the long game, filling the yolks of their eggs with cholesterol that would eventually destroy us.

Except then they weren't. It turned out that eggs were actually okay. Most of the cholesterol we were getting was created by our own bodies (betrayal!) when we ate

* Fun fact: Chickens, like all birds, do not have butts. They don't have genitalia. They just have one multipurpose hole called a *cloaca*, which handles the exit of pretty much anything that needs to exit their bodies.

foods like red meat. People could put away their nasty egg-white omelets and once again enjoy a real French omelet made from whole eggs the way that God intended. The chickens' master plan for our destruction was really not so bad after all. Except that it was. It turns out that much of our cholesterol is made by our own bodies, but that doesn't mean that we should be ingesting giant packets of the stuff in the form of egg yolks. Cholesterol is cholesterol, and in the United States, we eat so much that we can't afford to be adding more in any form. We should be avoiding sources of cholesterol to keep our hearts beating strongly through our retirements.

Except that eggs contain lots of good stuff, too. They're high in proteins that can help us stay full, reducing the likelihood that we overeat. Eating eggs early in the day results in fewer total calories consumed, which can lead to weight loss. Because obesity is tied to numerous causes of death that go far beyond just heart disease, the benefits of eggs outweigh the costs. We should all be eating them regularly, with gusto. Or should we? It's so hard to know.

STANDING IN THE CORNER

When I was a child, in addition to not thinking too much about eggs, I spent a lot of time in the corner. Not by choice, mind you. It was the place where my teachers often seemed to feel most comfortable with me. One minute, I would be enjoying life as a five-year-old. The next minute, for reasons that I often did not entirely understand, my teacher would be furiously standing over me, demanding that I go stand in the corner.

The walls of my preschool and, later, elementary school were made of cinder blocks. I don't remember many of the deeds that led to me occupying those corners, but I have clear memories of being so bored that I would trace the seams between the blocks with my eyes or my finger, pretending that they were rivers. I would spend my hours creating little maps, guiding expeditions through dangers untold and hardships unnumbered. Sometimes, after fifteen minutes or so, I'd be released from my adventures, allowed to return to the activities beyond my little corner. Other times, I would spend so much time in the corner that I would fall asleep. For reasons I still don't understand, this seemed to infuriate my teachers even more.

Occasionally, I would have the opportunity to bypass the corner altogether. Instead, I would be sent straight to Ms. Johnson's office. She was the director of the childcare center I attended. I had mixed feelings about her. She was often quite kind to me, but she was also a snitch. Upon arriving in her office, I always found her tattling to my mom about something I had done. She had never learned an important lesson that I imparted to my own classes once I became a teacher: Snitches get stitches.*

Things continued in this vein until second grade, when my teacher persuaded my parents to have me evaluated by a psychiatrist. The psychiatrist diagnosed me with attention deficit disorder (ADD). Although one of the most common diagnoses for children now, ADD (or ADHD as it began to be called in 1987) was rare enough in the mid-80s that my parents had never heard of it. Nor had they ever heard of Ritalin, the medicine the doctor prescribed for me.

My mom often describes the day I was diagnosed as one of the best days of her life. For years, she had been convinced that she was a bad mom. She was told that she should do a better job controlling me. Other times, it was simply implied that my challenging behavior was a result of her and my dad's poor parenting. The diagnosis suggested something else: that I was the way I was because of my weird brain. I think this also helped her reframe her reaction to my constant negative school reports. She went from feeling like I wasn't trying to understanding that I was trying my best, but my best was quite different from the "best" that her friends' children were capable of.

Most of the teachers I know went into education because of their positive experiences in classrooms. They were often the sweet little girls who could self-regulate through three-hour whole-group lessons. They got gold stars and pats on the head. Teachers loved them, and they loved teachers. When it came time to choose a career, they chose teaching because they wanted to become the teachers that they themselves had loved as children.

Not me. I became a teacher because I was treated so badly as a child. For circumstances beyond my control, I was hit, excluded, and yelled at. I was stigmatized as a troublemaker, my name passing from one teacher to another as one you didn't want in your classroom. I was "the bad kid in class." I became a teacher to provide a place where children like this were cared for and understood, where they could be held to high standards and taught, free from stigma and marginalization.

In the interest of being completely honest, I will tell you that I failed in this task my first year teaching. My preservice training had overwritten my original motivations and plans. As I was taught, so did I teach. I remember being intent on showing the

---

* The origin of this quote is debated, but I suspect it was originally coined by Brené Brown.

other teachers that I, even as a first-year teacher, would have full control over my class.* To that end, I saw success in straight lines and quiet mouths.

I would not remember my original motivation until my second year teaching, when I observed a teacher named Kim Hughes, who was the demonstration preschool teacher in my county. At this point in my career, I have observed more than one thousand classrooms, but Kim remains at the top of the list as the best teacher I have ever witnessed. She was effortless in her interactions with children, but everything ran smoothly. It was clear that she loved the children, and they loved her, and even though there were no stickers or card charts or clips or time-outs, everything still somehow went right. That classroom visit showed me how far I had to go to become an effective teacher. It also showed me that much of what I had learned about how to manage a classroom would have to be unlearned.

EGGS PART 2: THE CLOACA STRIKES BACK

This brings us back to eggs. Should we eat them? Should we not? It turns out that it's complicated. As I began to dive into understanding classroom management and challenging behavior, I found these topics to be complicated as well. One source would say one thing. The next one I read would completely contradict the first. I would attend professional development at school that told me to do XYZ, only to attend a different district-sponsored professional development at another school and have them tell me that XYZ would surely lead to the children's imminent destruction. As with the poultry ova conundrum, it's complicated.

Throughout my teaching career, I continued to search desperately for answers, and over time, I found them. I also decided that there was limited utility in following the advice of eighteen different conflicting sources, so I began to experiment in my classroom. I would try different approaches, collect data, and see what stuck. I would steal the best practices of teachers I admired and adapt those practices to work with my own style of teaching. By the time I left the classroom to go back to school for my PhD, my classroom really was one where all children, especially the squirrelly ones like young Adam, could thrive.

* My undergraduate degree was in elementary education. My first year in the classroom, I taught first grade. Then, I moved down to kindergarten, where I spent most of my teaching career. It was while I was teaching kindergarten that I returned to school for my master's degree in early childhood. After spending the next few years in kindergarten at a Reggio-inspired childcare center, and later in working with three-year-olds in an inclusive setting, I returned to school full-time on a fellowship to pursue my PhD. That is how I ended up where I am today, working at the University of North Carolina at Chapel Hill (UNC).

My doctoral program was where I started to understand the complex nature of challenging behaviors. As I read books and journal articles on theory and practice, light bulbs would often go on. I would finally understand why a certain practice worked or didn't work; why one approach insisted that I use it while another insisted that the other one would prove ruinous. I began to see the nuance. Sometimes, one practice might work well in the short term according to a particular framework, but another framework might show how that same practice could lead to long-term harms. Other times, a practice's benefits might outweigh the costs for some children but not for others. Because it's difficult to encapsulate that sort of nuance in a handy teacher's guide, that information is rarely included. Program creators will abandon gray accuracy in favor of less accurate black-and-white thinking, preferring "good enough" over a search for perfection. (Unfortunately, "good enough practice" doesn't roll off the tongue like "best practice," so everything just gets labeled as the latter.)

So, the first point of this book is to start untangling all of this a bit. We're going to talk about classroom practices in a way that hopefully contextualizes them and allows you to see clearly the costs and benefits so you can make informed decisions about when, where, and how to apply them. Eggs aren't good or bad. They probably shouldn't be the only thing you eat, but they have a role in a balanced diet. The different tools we have to address challenging behavior are similar. It's rarely this or that. It's *when* should I use this, or *with whom* should I use that. I'm going to assume that, if you're reading this, you are a professional who takes your own development as a teacher or administrator seriously, so while there are lots of ideas in this book, I will rarely tell you, "Do this exactly like this, or the children will revolt."

The second point of this book is to try to go beyond education theory. We will certainly bring in education theory perspectives, but I often worry that we are a little too siloed and insular in how we think about what we do in the classroom. After finishing my PhD, I have been fortunate to work with colleagues from many backgrounds outside the field of education: sociologists and economists, social psychologists and social workers. Over the years, their ideas have illuminated even more about why certain things in my classroom worked. They have also led to new ideas, which I have been able to try out secondhand as I coach teachers in implementing them.

In each chapter, I will present you with a new framework or theory. (Who wouldn't want to read about theory!?) Then, we'll explore how that theory plays out in the classroom, using it to understand why children act the way they do or why our actions affect them in a particular way. My hope is that these new lenses will allow you to see your classroom just a little bit differently. That way, when you're presented with a new challenge, and I'm not standing beside you telling you exactly what to do, you'll already understand how to adapt and solve the problem it presents.

During this journey, we'll electrocute pigeons in boxes,* explore how to put down rebellions, and dupe gullible Harvard students in the library. We'll explore our own brains, take a tennis lesson, discover why we're living in the golden age of colonoscopies, and discuss how to get people to invest in their 401(k)s. After exploring the origins and initial frameworks of these theories, we'll then apply them to classroom practice so you can feel confident using them in your own space with your own students.

GOING FOR A RUN

My first hope is that these new ways of seeing and thinking will open new ways for you to be with children. The word *motivate* comes from the Latin word for "to move," and a lot of what we talk about will focus on motivating kids. If we can't move kids, we can't teach them or effectively run a classroom. When we learn to move them, we become more effective teachers, which lets us be better at our jobs. That is, by the time children leave our classrooms, they will be further along in their developmental progression when we truly understand the sorts of topics we will talk about in this book.

This is not, however, all about the children. Teaching is a hard job, no matter what. I've worked in lots of fields, ranging from construction to restaurants to my current work as a researcher and implementation specialist at a major public university. Of all the things I've done, teaching is by far the most difficult. It is physically and mentally demanding in ways that other jobs cannot touch. (I suspect that those working in the medical field could give us a run for our money, but I have never worked in a hospital.) To be clear, nothing in this book is going to change that. However, as I began learning about the topics we will discuss in this book and applying them in my own kindergarten and preschool classrooms, this learning marked a turning point for me. Before, teaching had felt like walking into a windowless room to run on a treadmill. I would spend the day running faster and faster and faster just to keep up with the children. By the end of the day, I would be exhausted and disheartened, as I realized all that effort didn't move me forward a single inch. After, teaching felt more like going for a run on a nice spring day by a river. I would be exhausted at the end of the

* No pigeons were harmed in the writing of this book.

day, yes, but I would also feel like I had gone somewhere and seen some interesting things, like I had made some progress and moved forward. Teaching, I learned, can be incredibly fulfilling, even as I still found myself tired and full of questions more often than not.

My hope is that this book will do for you what the ideas in it did for me: lead you to a teaching practice that is effective and meaningful. No matter where you are in your teaching journey, we all deserve that, so buckle up and enjoy the ride. I am looking forward to this journey that we will take together.

—Adam

CHAPTER 1: CRAMMING PIGEONS INTO BOXES

The Ethics of Behaviorism

"

The most important human endeavor is the striving for morality in our actions. Our inner balance and even our very existence depend on it. Only morality in our actions can give beauty and dignity to life.

—ALBERT EINSTEIN, PHYSICIST

I took my first psychology course when I was a sophomore in college. Of all the things I learned, the one that sticks out the most is operant conditioning. The gist of the theory is that in the 1930s, a guy named B. F. Skinner* (1938) crammed a bunch of pigeons into boxes. On one side of the box was a green button. If the pigeon pushed the green button, a food pellet would be dispensed. On the other side of the box was a red button. If the pigeon pushed the red button, the box would be briefly electrocuted. After only a short time in the box, the pigeon would begin to repetitively press the green button and not so much as stray onto the side of the box with the red button.

Skinner theorized that to increase a behavior, you reward it, and to decrease a behavior, you punish it. This seems obvious now, but at the time, the idea was quite remarkable. Since Skinner's original intuitive leap, the theory has been broadly expanded. We now understand that consequences (rewards and punishments) are an incredibly powerful way to shape people's behavior. To this end, the theory has been fleshed out with numerous corollaries and sub-theories now accompanying it. The one that really sticks out from my psychology class was the power of intermittent rewards. That is, when rewards are only given occasionally and at random intervals, the desired behavior can be increased accordingly (Dragoi and Staddon, 1999). The picture in my psychology book featured a couple of women who looked like they were a combined four hundred years old, puffing on Virginia Slims, cranking down the handles of slot machines in an old-school Vegas casino.

Casinos may use the principle to lead people to hand over their hard-earned money, but I could list many other examples in which rewards and punishments have been used to shape people's behavior in positive ways. One of my friends works for a company that offers a prize each January, drawn at random, for employees who increase their 401(k) savings rate. The promise of a reward drives him and many of his colleagues to be more prepared for their retirement each year. I also frequently see police officers using radar to monitor car speeds on my way home. The threat of punishment in the form of a ticket keeps motorists driving more safely.

Since its inception in the early 1930s, behaviorism has steadily grown to become the dominant way that Americans understand motivation. We see it everywhere, from incentive packages in corporate America to punishments in our justice system to potty-training methods. In classrooms, punishments may range from being sent to the principal's office to detention to threats that one's relatives will

* For the record, Skinner looks exactly like you would think a psychology professor in the 1930s would: He's a white guy who wore horn-rimmed glasses and had a forehead large enough that you could project a movie onto it.

be called. Rewards may include the classic treasure box, verbal praise ("I like the way Dr. Holland is writing."), or [fill in the name of your school mascot] bucks. Some systems combine rewards and punishments. For example, children have clips with their names on them that can be moved up or down a stoplight or colored strip, depending on whether they are "good" or "bad."

For the record, all decisions we make in the classroom come with costs and benefits. If we teach children something in whole group, everyone gains from that instruction (a benefit!). However, it is difficult to effectively differentiate instruction in whole-group settings without some members of the class becoming bored, which in turn can lead to challenging behavior (a cost!). There is no One Practice to Rule Them All—no perfect way of doing things. Rather, it is our job as educators to maximize the benefits while minimizing the costs. To do so, we must have a strong understanding of those costs and benefits so we might choose intentionally what we wish to accomplish.

The benefits of behaviorism tend to be fairly well understood by the average American. Yet, we sometimes struggle as a society to understand the costs, so it's largely the costs that I want to discuss here. In this chapter, I will briefly discuss some ethical considerations that make using behaviorism in the classroom problematic. In the next chapter, I will introduce a more recent theory of motivation, self-determination theory (SDT), and use it to point out some of the efficacy downsides to behaviorism.

ETHICS VERSUS EFFICACY

When we talk about *ethics*, we are talking about what is morally right or wrong. In general, I think the field of education does a poor job separating the two. For example, many play advocates in the field feel that children have a moral right to play when they are young and should not be subjected to the drudgery of forced work at three or four years old. However, when they argue with policy makers and those seeking to push an academic curriculum down into preschools, they immediately move to an argument about *efficacy*: "Play is a phenomenal way to build language skills!" "Play teaches children how to work with others and builds social skills." "Play increases children's IQs!" These are all statements that appeal to the effectiveness of play in promoting other skills (and all are on shaky ground, research-wise; see Lillard et al., 2013 for a review). However, these individuals could just as easily make an argument based on ethics: "It's wrong to force four-year-olds to work on boring math worksheets because that is not how I would have wanted to be treated when I was four," is an appeal to an ethical argument, the so-called Golden Rule. Since I would argue that as education professionals, we have a duty to act ethically toward children, such appeals should not be minimized.

Let's say that, in the upcoming months after this book is released, a study will be published in a highly regarded, peer-reviewed journal. Because of the significance of its findings, the study will be cross-published in journals across multiple fields, ranging from education to child development to psychology. The study is rigorously done. Its sample is quite large and randomly drawn from the US population of four-year-olds. The children in the sample are randomly assigned to one of two conditions, allowing researchers not only to compare the groups but also to infer that the experimental condition is causing the differences between them. In short, the study has effectively minimized anyone's ability to critique its findings. That's important, because the findings of this study will certainly be controversial. In one of the conditions, the four-year-olds were taught basic math concepts exactly as their teachers were already planning to teach them. In the other, teachers did the same thing but with one addition: immediately prior to the lesson, the teachers struck their students on the heads with a half-inch-thick wooden dowel.* The surprising finding from the research was that students who were struck immediately prior to being taught math increased their math scores on several standardized, validated measures of math knowledge. In fact, the effect size was quite large. Children who were struck did much better than their un-struck peers; the approach produced a consistent outcome. Here's the question: knowing this, would you start beating children?

I often present this hypothetical situation to teachers, and, to their credit, they almost always unanimously suggest that they would not hit children with sticks. (Although, one time, I did see an administrator cross out the words *Home Depot* on his notes sheet.) The reason they tend to give is that beating children is wrong. It is unfair to beat children. Even individuals in favor of corporal punishment tend to shy away from hitting children who have done nothing wrong. Here, even though hitting children in the head yields some short-term benefits, the ethics and potential for long-term harm lead us to decide that we will not hit children with dowels before our math

---

*** This is the part where my lawyer would want me to tell you that this study is not real. I made it up to prove a point. Please do not start hitting children with sticks in the hope that they will be better counters.**

lessons. In this example, short-term efficacy (improved math learning) and the ethics (harm to children) of the situation are not compatible.

ETHICS AND (IN)CONSISTENCY

One ethical problem with the use of punishments and rewards in the classroom is that we are inconsistent in our use of them. Using these tools inconsistently sets up situations that are inherently unfair to some or all the children in our classrooms. Sometimes, teachers are intentionally inconsistent in their use of rewards and punishments; at other times, the inconsistency can be quite accidental.

Another thought exercise may be useful in helping us see how educators use operant conditioning inconsistently on purpose. Pretend you are a teacher and that you have a child in your class named Johnny. Johnny is . . . challenging. Each day, he comes in and spends his time hitting other children, talking when you are trying to talk, moving around on the carpet, and failing to complete his work. In short, Johnny makes your life a little more difficult every day, slowly draining your life force and leading you inexorably closer to what some might call a "drinking problem." On the other hand, you have another student in your class named Suzie. Suzie is the anti-Johnny. She is a delight to have in class. Each day, she comes in prepared to learn, acts politely toward others, and can self-regulate her way to the moon. She could sit stock-still for four hours listening to you drone on about the parts of a plant. Suzie reminds you of why you became a teacher in the first place.

One day, you bring the children in from the playground, help them get water, and then walk over to the carpet, where everyone is supposed to be seated and ready to start the next lesson. As you walk toward your chair, you notice that nearly everyone in your class is talking, playing, or rolling around. Getting their attention back will be easy enough. All you must do is tell them how much you like the way one of them is sitting, and within moments you can have them all staring up at you quietly. You look around to find someone. To your left, as always, is Suzie, sitting silently, with her hands in her lap. You glance to your right, and, in some sort of Festivus miracle, Johnny is also sitting quietly. Maybe he's tired from staying up too late the night before. Maybe he's distracted by a loose tooth. Maybe it's a new moon. For whatever reason, Johnny is a mirror image of Suzie. Now, we would all like to spend our days doing nothing but praising children for their excellent behavior, but your state has suggested that you also teach the children some things about letters and numbers and community helpers. Consequently, you only have time to like the way one child is sitting before moving on with the lesson. Given your time constraints, you need to decide whether you are going to praise Suzie or Johnny. So, who will it be? There is a correct answer, so take a moment to confer with a friend if you need to. Ready?

The correct answer here is Johnny. Nearly everyone gets this question right, even non-teachers. Why is Johnny the correct answer? Well, Johnny rarely has the opportunity to be praised at all, so we should take advantage of this once-in-a-lifetime chance! Once Johnny knows how nice it feels to be praised, he'll come back for more. As soon as he's hooked on our praise, Johnny will be easier for us to manage, he will experience more success in school, and we can get some of our life force back. Who is this not fair to? Suzie. She's being just as good as Johnny, but she isn't getting praised.

Now, I occasionally have people tell me that they think Suzie understands and that she is okay with this. She is not. A little parallel process might facilitate empathy for Suzie. Let's pretend for a moment that you are a good teacher. This will be easier for some of us than for others. (I'm kidding. You're all above average!) Every single day, you have interesting lessons planned, your students are engaged and ready to learn, and everything goes smoothly in your classroom. Down the hall is Ms. So-and-so. She couldn't teach her way out of a paper bag. Her students run wild, her lessons are boring, and you hate to even walk by her room because she yells at the children in what you originally assumed was a spot-on impression of Miss Trunchbull. One day, your administrator walks down the hall and peeks into your classroom. As always, you are killing it. Your students are doing an interesting hands-on lesson that integrates content across multiple subjects. Everyone is on-task and learning. Your administrator nods and then heads on down the hall. She gets to Ms. So-and-so's room. By virtue of an odd conjunction of the planets, Ms. So-and-so is also teaching an interesting lesson. For once, her students are on-task and doing what they're supposed to be doing. Your administrator nearly trips in her haste to close the door and run up to the office. Half out of breath, she gets on the intercom to the entire school and broadcasts this message: "I just want to take a moment to thank Ms. So-and-so. She is a real asset to our school, and I want to say how much I appreciate all of her hard work today." Your lip curls as you look up at the intercom in your room. All you can think is, "What?! She sucks! Why in the world are we interrupting our day to praise that no-teaching, grumpy old dumpster fire?!" That is how Suzie feels when you praise Johnny. But we do it, and we do it on purpose. It's not fair to Suzie, though. It's inconsistent, and because of this inconsistency, it's unethical.

Sometimes, we're inconsistent for reasons that I think of as being sort of accidental. Let's say I'm reading *Strega Nona* to the children. I get a few pages in, point to a character in a picture, and ask, "Who is this?" Carlos blurts out, "Big Anthony!" I say, "Ooh, Carlos, we're raising our hands before we answer." Then, I call on Esmerelda, who has her hand up, to tell me what Carlos already blurted out. We read a few more pages and I ask the children, "What just happened here?" Jane yells out, "Big Anthony didn't see her blow the kisses!" I wince and say, "Jane, I really need you to raise your hand if you want to speak." Then I call on Mekhi, who has his hand up, to tell me what Jane just blurted out. Each time someone just blurts out an answer, my cortisol level jumps up. Eventually, I ask the children, "Who can make a prediction about what will happen next?" Johnny blurts out, "Big Anthony isn't going to be able to stop the pasta!" It's too much. I look Johnny in the eye and say, "Johnny, I've warned you all twice already. Go move your clip!"

Do you see what happened here? Johnny just got punished for something that Carlos and Jane got away with. I didn't start the lesson intending to be inconsistent. In fact, being consistent would have been problematic. If I flipped the card or moved the clip of every child that ever called out in my kindergarten class, I quickly would have run out of cards to flip and places to move clips. Instead, our emotions often get the best of us, and we punish the third or fourth child who transgresses. We don't go into the lesson wanting to be inconsistent, but it happens all the time. Our use of rewards and punishments isn't fair. It's unethical.

Finally, we can frequently be inconsistent completely by accident. Teachers are like NFL referees. We often only see the second shove. At many points in my career, I have gone through periods of being a data collector on various research projects. I'm also an author on a classroom observation tool and have done even more observations in service of that tool's development and use. As part of these processes, I have been an observer in classrooms but also had discussions with other data collectors and members of my teams about what they see in classrooms. Whether it's me observing or one of my colleagues reporting on something, the view from the sidelines is a different perspective than being at the front of the room. When we're teaching, we are often so busy herding the cats that we miss important details about what is going on under our noses. This is not so when we are observing someone else.

A particular incident that sticks out in my memory occurred when one of my colleagues was observing in a second-grade classroom. Near the end of literacy center time, one of the students asked to go to the restroom in the back of the room. He cleaned up his center and headed in to take care of business. While he was there, the teacher called for the rest of the class to clean up and then line up to go outside. As is often the case for a group of seven- and eight-year-olds, the class was a little boisterous as they lined up to go to recess. The teacher, losing her temper just a bit, clapped and sharply admonished them that the next child who talked would be walking around a tree at recess.* You can probably guess what happened next. The child in the bathroom trundled out and found his place at the end of the line. He leaned over to the boy in front of him and whispered, "What did she say?" The other child turned back and whispered, "She said that if we talk, we have to walk around a tree." At that very moment, the teacher noticed the two boys breaking her hastily crafted rule and promptly relegated them to trees for the duration of their playtime.

I've yet to meet the adult who believes that these boys should have served the punishment they did. In a perfect world, the teacher would have recognized the extenuating circumstances surrounding the back-of-the-line whispering and reacted with leniency. Instead, caught up in the moment, she only saw what appeared to be a blatant disregard for her demand that the children remain silent in the line.

When I was a young preservice teacher, I learned that one of the attributes that excellent teachers possess is "with-it-ness," an ability to be aware of everything that is going on around them. I have no doubt that this particular attribute varies considerably within the teaching population. However, I also know that teachers with a flawless radar are nonexistent. No matter how hard we try, we will always run into situations in which we punish children who do not deserve it and reward children who deserve it even less. We will, despite our own best efforts, be inconsistent with our rewards and punishments. We will be unethical.

How this affects your practice depends on how you feel about the ethics of the situation. I know plenty of teachers who are okay with breaking a few eggs to make an omelet. Every practice in the classroom has costs and benefits, and being unethical to five-year-olds is a cost they're willing to pay, provided they maintain the control necessary to teach those five-year-olds what they need to know.

---

* Just to clarify for everyone who is mystified by this somewhat bizarre punishment: In the state where this occurred, teachers were not allowed to prevent children from engaging in physical activity during recess. What is a teacher in need of punishment options to do? Require the student to orbit a tree rather than playing with his friends.

SCAFFOLDING

I am generally not in favor of using rewards and punishments as a blanket classroom management tool for both ethical and efficacy reasons, which we will discuss in other chapters. However, that is not to say that I never use them. For children who need to get their foot on the bottom rung of the ladder, they can be a powerful short-term tool. One first-grade teacher with whom I worked was blessed by her principal with every child who had serious behavior issues in kindergarten. She started her year intending not to use rewards and punishments but found that her class could not even get to the carpet in the morning without a fight breaking out. What to do? She grabbed her trusty pompom jar, told the kids that when they filled it to the line, they could have a party, and started dropping pompoms in every time they transitioned quietly. A week or so later, one of the children turned to her while heading to the carpet to begin the morning and said, "This is really nice. We should come to the carpet like this every day." They had a discussion about it, agreed that they should be able to do this without the jar, and she removed it from the room later that week. (They had the party they had been saving up for as a celebration.)

Rewards and punishments can be an effective tool for individual children who need a little extra assistance. For children who need extra intervention, rewards can be a powerful motivator to begin enacting a desired behavior. Behavior plans and token economies can be used to help a child form a habit that will provide them with greater happiness and success in life. In both the case of the individual teacher and that of the individual child, however, behavior plans and other instances of behaviorism in the classroom should be seen as scaffolding in the classic Brunerian* sense of the word. That is, scaffolding provides additional support to help children develop a skill that they cannot do on their own. Where we often go wrong with this both in school and wider society, is that we tend to leave the scaffolding up far too long. In the real world, scaffolding is necessary to build many buildings. However, we would never think of leaving it up after the building was complete. In classroom after classroom, however, I walk in and see permanent scaffolding erected at the front of the class in the form of card and clip charts, pompom jars, and [fill in the name of your school mascot] bucks. Scaffolding that remains past its usefulness makes for ugly buildings and ugly classrooms. So, whenever I work with teachers to put behavior plans in place, I also work with them to create an exit strategy. At what point

---

* Jerome Bruner coined the term *scaffolding*, and for those who are wondering, he looked like the grandpa you always wished you had.

will we know if the plan is working? If the plan is working, how will we begin paring down the use of behaviorism? These are important questions to think about before teachers even start using behaviorism to shape children's behavior, but they are rarely considered.

The final ethical appeal I want to make around behaviorism goes back to a basic ethical principle: the Golden Rule. The version I grew up with (in the American South) was, "Do unto others as you would have them do unto you." Let's do a little thought experiment to illustrate how this could play out in a parallel process. In your place of employment, your boss puts up a clip chart. There are colors going up and down a strip and clothespins attached to it with each employee's name on a clothespin. When your boss sees an employee doing something she likes, she gets on the intercom, announces to everyone that she likes the way so-and-so is teaching/administrating/working, and then has so-and-so come up to the office to move her clip. Conversely, whenever she notices that someone is doing something she doesn't like, she gets on the intercom and says, "So-and-so, you know you're not supposed to be ______. Come up to the office and move your clip down." If so-and-so has her clip moved down enough times, she will of course have to call her mother/father/caregiver to explain herself.

I always think this scenario sounds a little funny when I present it, but I also recognize that it would enrage and demean me if I actually worked under it. Even initiatives that smell like this—such as contract renewal and merit pay being dependent on test scores— universally tend to anger educators. So, why do we continue to subject children to these systems? Even if they are effective at gaining us the compliance we desire in the short term, we would generally abhor these practices if they were applied to us. To be better, we have to start treating children the way we would want to be treated if we were in their little shoes.

* * *

In summary, behaviorism is an extremely effective way to gain children's compliance in the short term but is problematic for two key ethical reasons. First, educators apply behaviorism in an inconsistent manner both intentionally and unintentionally, frustrating some children while rewarding the undeserving. Second, educators do things to children to promote good behavior that they would never allow to be done to themselves. Thus, they violate the Golden Rule. Whether you are comfortable doing these things despite this ethical dilemma is not a decision I can make for you. Rather, I want to provoke some thought about this issue, as it is one we frequently gloss over in our attempts to improve our practice. Let us not stop here, though, as our next chapter will begin to confront some of the long-term issues with employing behaviorism as a means of addressing challenging behavior.

CHAPTER 2: THE MATTHEW CLUB

Meeting Children's Universal Needs

Revenge is a dish best served cold.

—ANCIENT KLINGON PROVERB

My first year teaching, a group of my students attempted to destroy me. I know that teachers sometimes jokingly say things like that. My six-year-old students had a plan in mind. It took me a long time after that first year to figure out where I had gone wrong, but eventually I found the reasons in a theory from the field of cognitive psychology called *self-determination theory* (SDT). SDT was created by a pair of psychologists named Richard Ryan and Ed Deci (2000). In addition to showing me where I went wrong my first year, this theory ended up informing my later understandings about what works to effectively handle challenging behavior in a classroom. I owe a lot to these two gentlemen and the myriad researchers who have worked over the last forty or fifty years to validate and expand their theory. In this chapter, I am going to cover the basics of the central part of the theory—universal needs—and then talk about how the theory can be applied to classroom practice. In doing so, I hope to highlight some of the problems with using behaviorism if one is not mindful of the long-term consequences.

SELF-DETERMINATION THEORY IN A NUTSHELL

According to SDT, development is an active process. It does not occur entirely within the individual. It is not wholly impacted by the environment. Instead, development occurs at the intersection between the two. To develop in an optimal way, individuals must fulfill their basic needs. For a long time, scientists have been solid on physiological needs: All humans need food. All humans need water. All humans need sleep. If you live somewhere like Michigan or Vermont or Svalbard, you need shelter. When the environment fulfills these needs, we achieve optimal development, improved functioning, and a positive sense of well-being. When the environment fails to fulfill these needs, we experience the other side of these outcomes: poor development, difficulty functioning, and unhappiness.

We can see how this failure to fulfill needs plays out when we look at food. Children who are malnourished are, to understate the point, not experiencing a positive sense of well-being. I get miserable and hungry when I fast for a day, so I cannot even imagine what it feels like to go a week without food. The misery that accompanies chronic malnourishment is hugely problematic. Development is also negatively affected across a variety of domains. Obviously, physical development is stunted. Malnourished children tend to be smaller in terms of both height and weight than their well-fed peers. There are a host of other physical problems that come along with poor nourishment such as impaired fine and gross motor skills. Malnourished children have lower bone density and muscle tone. Cognitive development is similarly stunted. Malnourished children tend to have lower IQs than their well-fed peers. Even social and emotional development are stunted. Malnourished children tend to have lower levels of social competence than their well-fed peers.

In some places, children can be malnourished but still have food around them in the environment. This is particularly a problem in highly developed countries, where family poverty or neglect can exist right down the street from a grocery store filled with food. In cases like this, children will often develop what are known as *maladaptive behavioral patterns* to fulfill their needs. That is a fancy way of labeling a behavior that fulfills a need in the short term but can be problematic in the long term. For example, if a child is not receiving enough food, they may turn to theft to fulfill their need. Children who steal food also often hoard or binge their ill-gotten gains. In the short term, stealing food helps children fulfill their need, but in the long term, theft is not a great habit to take on. It is also worth noting here that maladaptive behavioral patterns tend to be very persistent. Children who steal and hoard food often continue to do so even after their circumstances improve and they consistently receive adequate food.

As I noted, our understanding of universal physical needs existed long before Ryan and Deci created SDT. What Ryan and Deci brought to the table is the idea that, in addition to universal *physiological* needs, we also have universal *psychological* needs that follow basically the same pattern. First, to qualify as a universal psychological need, a need has to exist across cultures. If Americans desire it but members of the !Kung-San people in the Kalahari Desert do not, it is not a universal need. Second, the need must be something that persists across the lifespan. Many infants and toddlers enjoy eating a nice handful of beach sand. However, most of my friends in their thirties and forties have kicked the beach-sand habit, so beach sand is not a universal need.

Finally, to qualify as a universal need, the fulfillment of the need has to promote positive development and improved functioning, and to increase one's sense of well-being in the long term. This unfortunately rules out money. I say *unfortunately* because, although I am not an aggressive player by any means, I fully intend to win the lottery one day. On the rare occasion that I buy a ticket, I will often daydream about diving in and out of a giant pile of money like Scrooge McDuck while my nephews run off and get into mischief with Launchpad McQuack. However, research on lottery winners suggests that they receive about a six-month boost to their sense of well-being before reverting to their original levels of happiness. If you find this as depressing as I do, recognize that the opposite is also true. Individuals who have a limb amputated tend to suffer from a decreased sense of well-being for about six months before reverting to their original levels. Money and limb possession simply do not qualify as universal needs.

At this point, a significant amount of research supports the existence of three universal needs: autonomy, relatedness, and competence. Just so we are all clear on what these mean, I will briefly define them. *Autonomy* refers to people's ability to be in control of their own lives. When we feel like we are making choices on our own behalf rather than being forced into situations, we develop optimally and experience a heightened sense of well-being. For example, teachers who teach in schools with scripted curricula enjoy their jobs less than their peers in schools where teachers have autonomy to plan and implement their own lessons. Scripted-curricula teachers experience a decreased sense of well-being because they lack autonomy at work.

Relatedness refers to the fact that we desire a positive relationship with those around us. Think about some of your past jobs. In some, everyone you worked with was a pig-faced, smelly fathead. Just being around those people caused you to lose a little hair and sanity. In other jobs, you probably got along well with your colleagues. You had positive relationships, both in and outside the school or office. When you needed something, you felt supported by your boss and colleagues. If you had to go back and do one job again, which would you choose? When our need for relatedness is fulfilled, we experience optimal functioning and enhanced well-being, just like you no doubt did in that second workplace.

Finally, *competence* refers to our need to succeed at the tasks we undertake. When babies are first born, they possess what is known as *effectance motivation*. They simply want to have an effect on the world. However, quite early, this need transitions into a need to not only affect things around us but also to succeed at achieving a goal. When given puzzle pieces, children as young as two exhibit a desire to assemble the pieces correctly or make them fit into the correct little slots. My first couple of years teaching, I struggled with classroom management. I woke up every day dreading having to go to school and do battle with my students. As I learned how to teach in more engaging ways and how to manage my classroom more effectively, I began to look forward to each new day with the children. As my competence increased, so did my sense of well-being and intrinsic motivation. I suspect that it is the same for you. In years when your plans have gone well and the children have been receptive to your teaching, you feel better about your job, you function more effectively, and you improve your practice more easily.

In the previous chapter, I discussed some of the ethical issues with using behaviorism in the classroom. In this chapter, I want to talk about efficacy. In short, although behaviorism is extremely effective at gaining short-term compliance from children, it has some long-term consequences related to children's need fulfillment that prove problematic. Several features of behaviorism serve to frustrate children's abilities to fulfill their needs in schools and classrooms. This, in turn, leads to a reduction in the sense of well-being, intrinsic motivation, and the development of those pesky maladaptive behavioral patterns. Again, I want to reiterate that this does not mean you should avoid using behaviorism altogether. Rather, you should be intentional about its use, balancing the positive things that it gets you with the potential downsides for children's long-term development.

AUTONOMY

Let's talk about the need for autonomy first. If autonomy is having control over one's own experiences and actions, then the opposite of autonomy is being controlled by others.* By their very nature, rewards and punishments are used to manipulate others into doing things they wouldn't normally do. If they would already engage in an activity, then there is no real reason to use a reward or punishment. Therefore, manipulating children using rewards and punishments sets us up to frustrate their ability to fulfill their need for autonomy.

Children often struggle to articulate complex psychological processes like this, so I will turn once again to my own experience to illustrate how this feels. At some point during my teaching career, the principal at my school went to a "How to be a Good Principal" workshop of some form or another. One of the tidbits that she picked up was the idea that letting teachers know how much you appreciate them would lead to improved staff morale and, I am sure, several other positive outcomes. My principal came back to school and put into action this tidbit by altering the email signature that automatically went out at the bottom of each one of her emails. She changed her usual sign-off from Sincerely, Jane McPrincipal to read, "Thanks for all you do!" followed by her name and the school's contact information. Any time she sent an email out to anyone at the school, we would instantly be thanked. The problem with

* My eleventh-grade English teacher would be screeching right now over the passive verb tense I used in the previous sentence. In this case, though, the passive verb points to the issue here: Without autonomy, we are passive beings. With autonomy, we are active participants in shaping our own lives.

this little maneuver was that, occasionally, I would get emails that read something like this:

> Dear Mr. Holland,
>
> I noticed when I came into your room today to observe writing that you spent an extra seven minutes on the playground with the children. This sort of action is completely unacceptable. You are wasting the time of your students and myself. I would be more than happy to help you find gainful employment elsewhere.
>
> Thanks for all you do!
>
> Jane McPrincipal

I would read emails like this and immediately begin to seethe. The body of the email is bad enough, but what really made me grind my teeth was the sign-off. She doesn't thank me for all I do! She doesn't respect me as a professional. That fact was evident based on the body of the email, and the juxtaposition of the body and the sign-off just served to highlight the fact that she was attempting to manipulate me (and the rest of the staff) into believing that we were cared about and valued as partners in educating children.

Confronted with the evidence of my principal infringing on my autonomy, there were two ways that things could have gone, just like with children: I could have experienced a decreased sense of well-being at my job and decreased intrinsic motivation around my teaching, or I could find a maladaptive way to fulfill my need for autonomy.* When our classrooms do not fulfill children's need for autonomy, teachers will experience similar results: children who enjoy school less and are less intrinsically motivated *or* students who push back against our attempts at control. When we use rewards and punishments to gain control over our classes, this is inevitably where we end up.

RELATEDNESS

In addition to creating an environment that frustrates children's ability to fulfill their need for autonomy, rewards and punishments also create one that frustrates children's ability to fulfill their need for relatedness. To understand why, it is helpful

* Spoiler alert: We stayed out an extra ten minutes the next day.

to look at an interesting study conducted by James Heyman and Dan Ariely (2004) in the field of behavioral economics. In one study, the researchers asked participants to do a mind-numbing computer task: dragging balls that appeared on the left side of a computer screen into a square on the right side. Some participants received a little compensation for their work. Others received greater compensation. Unsurprisingly, the participants who received more money for their drudgery dragged more balls into the square. The twist here comes in the third condition, in which there was no compensation offered. A research assistant merely asked the participants to drag as many balls as they could into the square. Interestingly, the participants in this condition dragged more balls into the square than in either of the conditions where the participants were paid.

When we think back to what we know about behaviorism, this finding is counterintuitive. Shouldn't the rewards promote more of the desired behavior of ball dragging? In this case, it appears that SDT does a better job of helping us understand what is occurring here. When participants were offered money, they entered into what was clearly an economic relationship. When the participants were asked by the research assistant to drag as many balls as they could, they were fulfilling the request because of a social relationship, even if it was a tenuous one. After all, helping those around us is one of the key ways that we build rapport. The offer of the reward changes the fundamental underlying nature of our relationships with those around us from a social one into an economic one.

This is pretty evident in schools, too. As I am observing classes for my work, I will often be walking behind a group of students in the hallway at the beginning of the year, and the teacher will notice that someone's shoe is untied. Not wanting to stop the line and tie the shoe herself (a smart move, as I have found that such laces are often soaked in urine), she asks if anyone in the class knows how to tie shoes. One or two children proudly raise their hands. The selected child will then step out of line with their floppy-shoelaced friend, tie the shoe, and rejoin the line farther down the hall. The reasons that children help tie shoes in these situations are all good ones. They enjoy feeling competent at something. They care about their friends and do not want them to fall down. They have a relationship with the teacher and want to be helpful to her. Fast forward a few months. In the interim, someone at the school decided that we should make an effort to "catch children being good." Being thus caught will, of course, be rewarded with [fill in the name of your school mascot] bucks. After this program goes into effect, when I am walking down the hall behind the class, the teacher will notice another child with an untied shoelace. She'll ask if anyone can help. Immediately, nine children dive to the ground. Elbows fly and a scrum ensues. After all the eye gouging and biting is over, the "winning" child grips his friend's shoelaces and yells up to the teacher while tying, "LOOK AT ME! I'M BEING GOOD!" All the reasons for engaging in the helpful behavior have changed because the underlying nature of the relationship has changed. The teacher is now the reward-giver. Other children are competition for those economic rewards. It is now difficult for children to fulfill their need for relatedness with either the teacher or one another because of their involvement in this newly created economy. As we can see here, their intrinsic motivation to engage in altruistic behavior has been, predictably, diminished.

All of this brings us back to my first year of teaching. When I graduated from college, behaviorism was the only method I knew for classroom management. To that end, it was all behaviorism all the time. My school had a card chart system in which each child in the class had a pocket containing cards of different colors. The front card was yellow, the best color according to our completely arbitrary color system. Behind that card was a blue one. Behind the blue card was a pink card. Behind the pink card was the dreaded green card. If a child was caught being bad, I would tell them to go flip their card to the next color down. At the end of the day, I would report behavior to parents based on the card color. Other consequences were also tied to the cards, ranging from silent lunch to walking laps at recess. The problem with the card system was that children could only go down and not up. If you flipped your card to blue, there was no way to get back to yellow, per our school policy. To add a positive spin, I created a Star Chart. Children could move from Shining Star to Super Star, or alternatively, they could drop off the chart if they were "bad." The chart had stickers and glitter and streamers. It took my assistant almost a full day to make it. I accompanied these tools with other rewards such as Fun Friday and extra recess. I constantly said I liked the way children were sitting. I look back on all of this with a certain amount of regret, of course, but I also didn't know any better. I didn't understand the impacts these rewards and punishments were having on my students.

That first year, I saw my chief mission as teaching the North Carolina Standard Course of Study for first grade. I had a pile of knowledge, and my job was to deliver it into my students' heads. When students misbehaved, they prevented me from doing my job. I would respond with my behaviorism tools. I would "like" the way the children next to them were sitting. I would threaten to flip cards or call parents/grandparents/aunts/uncles/dogs. I would offer Fun Friday for children who could get through a day on Super Star. In short, I was moving in one direction, teaching my curriculum, and when children would pop up and obstruct me, I would move them out of the way so I could continue.

My most frequent obstructions were a group of five boys. Managing them was like playing a game of whack-a-mole. As soon as I would get one of them settled, another would pop up to obstruct my mission. It was not until December that I came to understand that this pattern was not coincidence. Things came to a head one morning when the mother of one of these boys, Trey, arrived in my classroom before school and asked to sit down with me for a chat. I pulled her up an adult-sized chair next to my desk and asked what I could do for her. She told me, "Trey's father and I sat down with him last night and asked him why he has been getting in so much trouble in Mr. Holland's room. Trey told us that the reason is 'Matthew Club.'" One of the children in my class was named Matthew, but I had no idea what she was talking about, so I asked her, "Do you happen to know what Matthew Club is?" She said, "Oh yes," and proceeded to pull out a notebook that she began to read to me: "The point of Matthew Club is to be bad and not listen to Mr. Holland." My cortisol level went through the roof, but I tried to keep it together because there was a parent in the room, so I calmly asked her, "You wouldn't happen to know who's in Matthew Club by any chance, would you?" She said, "Of course. I wrote them down," and she read off the names of these five boys, "Matthew, Isaiah, Drew, Seth, and Trey." I began taking deep breaths and counting in my head. I kept an even tone as I thanked her for coming and let her know that we would take care of it.

As soon as she walked around the corner in the hallway, I stormed down to my mentor Melissa's room. "You are not going to believe what I just found out," I seethed, flop sweat dripping down the side of my face. "Apparently, there is a club in my classroom, the point of which is to be bad and not listen to me! I'm going to call Matthew's grandfather so he can come down here and take care of him!" Melissa looked me dead in the eyes and said, "You need to calm down. You are a twenty-two-year-old man with a degree from Wake Forest University and all the power and resources of the Wake County Public School system behind you. You need to start your own club and steal all of his friends."

My eyes lit up. This was so brilliant. It was December. We were already planning to make papier-mâché snowmen. I skipped back up the hall and whistled as I stirred up the glue water and inflated the balloons.

When my students arrived, we sat down for morning meeting and I told them, "I'm so excited that you're here today, because I have really exciting news! I'm starting my own club, the Mr. Holland Club, the point of which is to be good and listen to Mr.

Holland. If you're part of my club, we have some fun things planned." As my assistant brought out the balloons, glue water, and newspapers, the kids started drooling. I said, "There are some rules, though. The first rule of Mr. Holland Club is you do not talk about Mr. Holland Club. The second rule of Mr. Holland Club is you do not talk about Mr. Holland Club. (Don't worry if this *Fight Club* reference went right over your head. It was lost on my six-year-olds as well.) The last rule of Mr. Holland Club is that you can't be in any other clubs. Now, everyone who wants to join Mr. Holland Club, grab a balloon!" As my class ran to grab balloons, I looked those five boys dead in the eye and said, "Slow down." They looked longingly on at the other children as they cut up newspaper and splashed around in the glue water. After a minute or two, I called Trey. He toddled over to me and I said, "Hey buddy, you don't really want to be in Matthew Club, do you?" He vigorously shook his head no. I said, "You want to be in Mr. Holland Club, don't you?" He gave an equally vigorous nod yes. I said, "Grab a balloon, buddy!" I waited another minute and then called Seth over; another minute and called Drew over; another minute and called Isaiah over, until finally Matthew was sitting on the carpet all by himself. In that moment, I knew that I had won and we would not have any issues for the rest of the year.

Those of you who have been teaching for a while are probably shaking your heads right now. Like most first-year teachers, I was blessedly naïve. The rest of the year proceeded much as the first semester had gone, with Matthew and company remaining a thorn in my side. For many years after this occurred, I blamed Matthew for this whole incident. I mean, what kind of jerk six-year-old starts a club to overthrow his teacher? Now, however, having the benefit of hindsight and some more experience, I can see that this was my fault. I had put myself on one team and these boys on another team. Matthew was just the smartest of the bunch and the only one to realize what I had done. Once he understood the role I had assigned him, he played it to the hilt.

COMPETENCE

Looking back on my teaching career, I have regrets (as I imagine all teachers do). The way I handled these five boys marks my single greatest one. Each one of these boys arrived in first grade wanting to have a good experience. Each one of these boys wanted to have an enjoyable year. Each one of these boys wanted school to be a place where he belonged. As the teacher, it was my job to fulfill those wishes, and I failed.

I failed miserably. My failure was certainly not the result of maliciousness on my part but of ignorance. Still, every time I think about that first year, I wish for a do-over.

At no point, in any of my "liking" or threatening to call parents or denying children access to Fun Friday or card flipping did I ever do anything to fulfill these boys' need for relatedness. Instead, I created a classroom ruled by economic relationships and then, due to their inability to meet my expectations, I denied them any of the economic rewards that might have come out of those relationships. Please note that word: *inability*. I am quite sure that each one of those boys arrived on their first day of school with the motivation to behave. Six-year-olds do not lie in bed the night before the first day of school thinking, "I really hope I'm the bad kid in class this year," or, "I hope that my inability to control my impulses leads to me being ostracized by my peers and teacher." They lie there thinking, "Man, I really hope my teacher likes me this year," or, "I sure do hope I make lots of friends tomorrow." Children come in with the *motivation* to do what we want but often lack the *ability*. When we rely heavily on rewards and punishments, we run the risk of frustrating their ability to fulfill their needs, which leads to decreased motivation, even as they begin to gain more ability. In the end, this leads to children whose behavior gets worse over the course of the year, even as their brains develop and they have more chances to practice, indicating that we should see behavior improvements.

* * *

With that, I'll conclude my description of children's psychological needs. The universal needs for autonomy, relatedness, and competence will serve as the basis for much of my discussion about children's motivation as I talk about how to address challenging behavior. In short, effective classroom management in this framework is about fulfilling children's needs to promote long-term success while finding ways to ensure that we are meeting our own short-term goals. But before diving into practical application of relationship-based methods, I would like to devote one more chapter to SDT and the idea that not all motivation is created equal.

CHAPTER 3: COPY MACHINES

Types of Motivation

Motivate from Latin *movere:*
"to move"

B. F. Skinner (1987) went to his grave arguing that the only thing scientists should be studying in people was behavior, suggesting that study of emotions and thoughts was completely irrelevant and unnecessary. He felt the need to argue this because of a rise in interest in emotions and our underlying thinking. You see, although behavior was the focus for many years in psychology because of Skinner's breakthroughs, scientists began to find that behaviorism couldn't explain a number of findings in the social sciences. For example, behaviorism suggests that the stronger a punishment, the greater the effect and the less likely the individual is to repeat the behavior. Consequently, the American justice system embraced stronger punishments for a variety of crimes. Puzzlingly, however, these greater punishments did not appear to reduce the likelihood of criminals repeating their crimes after they left prison. Because of this and a number of other situations where behaviorism failed to adequately explain or predict people's behavior, scientists began to suspect that human brains might be more complex than those of Skinner's pigeons. Moreover, they began to wonder if that greater complexity might make a difference.

Self-determination theory (SDT), which we covered in the last chapter, was one of a number of theories that arose in the 1960s and 1970s seeking to explore how human thoughts and emotions might influence behavior and action in different ways. We have already discussed how universal human needs can affect growth, development, and behavior. Another, related sub-theory in this framework deals with how different motivations might affect how humans act.

Put simply, Ryan and Deci (2000) argued that not all motivation is created equal. Originally, they suggested that motivation would fall into two categories: intrinsic and extrinsic. Over time, Deci and Ryan (1985) used the results from hundreds of studies to revise their theory to reflect a continuum of different types of motivation. The continuum ranges from behavior that is completely non-self-determined and behavior that is entirely self-determined. I won't go through each point on the continuum, but I think that looking at a few of the positions can give us an idea of how the theory shakes out and why it might be useful in our classrooms.

THE CONTINUUM OF MOTIVATION

At one end of the continuum is amotivation. We can all think of a time when we asked a child to do something and they looked us dead in the eye and said, "No." That child was amotivated; literally, not moving. At the opposite end of the continuum is intrinsic motivation. The term *intrinsic motivation* is often misused in pop culture, so I want to be sure to define it here. Within SDT, *intrinsic motivation* refers to any behavior or activity where the reward is the activity itself. We all have activities we enjoy doing just because we enjoy doing them: reading books, rock climbing, or gardening.* I personally like to think of myself as an avid napper who is only retaining his amateur status because of his love of the game. No one has to pay us to do these things. My wife never has to nag me to get me to play video games. We are intrinsically motivated to do these things, making the behavior entirely self-determined.

Sitting in the gulf between amotivation and intrinsic motivation are a variety of types of motivation that are all tied to external prompts or sources. We do these things not because we enjoy them and decided to do them but because some external source or motivation prompts us to do so. The honest truth is that a vast majority of the activities that occur in our classrooms and our lives fall into these categories, so it pays to have a good understanding of them and what they mean for children's behaviors.

Down at the end of the continuum next to amotivation is extrinsic external motivation. If you're thinking that's a lot of words with the *ex-* prefix, you're right. We engage in these behaviors entirely as a response to an outside demand. Take a moment, wherever you are right now, and stand up. Go ahead. Stand up. I know some of you are ignoring this. Stop ignoring this. Stand up. I'm really not going to stop bothering you until you do. Alright. Are you standing? If you still aren't standing, stop being the last holdout and stand up.** Okay, now sit back down. I would love to tell you that the reason I had you stand was because I care deeply about your health or preventing deep vein thrombosis or some such nonsense. That would be a lie. I only had you stand up to prove a point.

The only reason you stood up is because I told you to. I know nothing about your current situation or position. I don't care about your deep vein thrombosis. You were unlikely to be on the cusp of standing up anyway. You only stood because of that external prompt. Based on my pilot testing of this, I can characterize your behavior as likely being begrudging. Even when I do this in person, I see a lot of people looking around to see if other people are standing up. The whole exercise takes about fifteen

---

* Sometimes, when I present this, someone tentatively raises their hand and offers up more daring intrinsically motivated activities, such drinking alcohol or S-E-X, and we all titter like schoolgirls.

** I'm very sorry to the two of you who stood up immediately and to those of you who were already standing. Pilot testing has suggested that some people need a lot of prompting.

seconds because I refuse to stop nagging until nearly everyone is on their feet. In the end, however, social pressure gets nearly everyone up.

This sort of begrudging compliance is exactly what we tend to see when motivating people via external regulation. It's barely more than going through the motions. Moreover, when people run into a snag, they tend to give up easily. If we take a moment to reflect on our classrooms, we can think of plenty of times when we motivate children this way. It is, after all, the fastest way to get children moving (or stopping). "James, stop running in the classroom." "Jodi, be quiet in the hallway." "Jamal, don't lie down in that puddle in the bathroom." In each of these cases, we provide an external prompt that results in compliance. But I wonder if you have ever noticed the type of compliance you receive. In my personal experience, like those of you slowly standing, the compliance is often begrudging. Moreover, such requests often don't change children's long-term behavior. That is, children tend not to value and internalize behaviors that they engage in solely to comply with external requests, so we have to ask again and again and again until we lose our tempers and point out that we've asked a hundred times for the behavior we want. Here's the thing: Children react like all people do to this kind of motivation, so the blame falls squarely on us. We can't expect young children to do more than adults could. (Research suggests that repeated requests of this sort in the workplace yield unengaged workers as well. See, for example, Ryan and Deci, 2000; Singh, 2016.)

So we move up the motivation continuum away from external extrinsic motivation and toward intrinsic motivation. One step up from this is introjected external regulation.* We are motivated in this way when we do something out of guilt or to boost our fragile egos. Sometimes, when I am at my busiest, someone will ask me to read something they are writing about classroom management, because I have some expertise there. I don't want to do it, but I do anyway because they called me an expert. (How could I resist?!) Here, the prompt for doing the activity is external, but it's supported by something internal (my feelings of guilt or pride). Those feelings, however, are still not tied to the task itself. Doing something out of guilt generally doesn't cause us to give it our all, but our participation is usually stronger than if someone just told us to do the task.

I don't see this type of motivation happen in the classroom too often, but it does come up occasionally. Teachers will say, "Cruz, what would your mother say if she saw you doing X," prompting Cruz to stop doing X to avoid those feelings of guilt. It's more

---

* I sometimes think it would kill a psychologist to use normal, human language to name things. *Introjected*?

effective than just telling Cruz to stop doing X, but we still aren't into the best that extrinsic motivation has to offer. That is reserved for our next two types.

The last two types, identified and integrated extrinsic motivation, are what researchers consider the more optimal ways to motivate others. With both motivation types, the impetus or drive behind the behavior is something external to the behavior itself, but we still internally value the behavior despite that. I often think of this type of motivation when I am wrist deep in toilet water, scrubbing out my bathroom. No one I know derives any joy from cleaning a toilet or scrubbing a shower, but we sure enjoy the clean bathroom we get as a result of the work. We identify with the need for the task. There are many times when we are externally prompted to do something, but we also identify with and understand the why of the task. I think exercise is another classic example. Running is miserable. It's painful at worst and monotonous at best.* We run because it makes us look and feel a certain way that we like when the run is over.

This isn't just an "ends justify the means" sort of argument. For children, in particular, there is a process to socialization in which external rules, guidelines, and values gradually become internalized. What I mean is that we have to tell very young children to be quiet in a theater. Over time, they come to understand the reason behind the request and believe in it as their own value. What was once an external command gradually becomes internalized.

In the classroom, there are many times when we wish children to internalize our own beliefs and values. We want children to be safe, so we require walking feet in the classroom. It is our desire that children would eventually walk rather than run because they believe this too, rather than continually having to prompt them to walk. I want to focus on this, because good classroom management isn't only about gaining compliance in the moment. It is about helping children to internalize the values and beliefs that will promote their success later in life.

The reason that I'm bringing all of this up now is that the likelihood that children will internalize these values and beliefs changes, depending on the kind of motivation that children experience with respect to our rules and procedures. The closer to intrinsic motivation we get on the scale, the more likely children are to internalize the behavior. The reason for this is what researchers call *locus of control* (not to

---

* I can already feel some of you brimming with outrage here. "But, but, but, I love running! My runner's high," etc. Bless your hearts, we are all entitled to our own opinions about running. It's important to keep in mind here that mine is right and yours is wrong.

be confused with the heavy metal band, Locusts on Command). *Locus of control* refers to whether we feel like we're doing something because we want to or because something external has made us do it. When children feel like they're doing something because they want to do it, they're more likely to do it again without prompting. "After all," they think, "I have chosen to do this." On the other hand, when children only do something for external reasons, they are less likely to internalize the behavior. "After all," they think, "I am only doing this because I have to."

This holds true whether the external prompt is a simple command, a command with a threat of punishment, or a command with the possibility of a reward for compliance. Let's think about the reward scenario for a moment, as it is the most frequently used motivator in schools currently. The teacher asks the children to line up quietly and tells them that she will give a Dingo Dollar to each child who does so. The children line up silently and the teacher passes out the Dingo Dollars. *In the moment*, the teacher has gotten exactly what she wants: a quiet line. The trouble, of course, is the long-term consequence of her action. She now has a class full of children who are thinking to themselves, "The reason I line up quietly is to get Dingo Dollars." For many of these children, there is no reason to line up quietly if Dingo Dollars aren't being offered. This is especially problematic because some of those children had probably already internalized the rule. They saw the value of lining up quietly. But that value has now been replaced by the more salient and enticing Dingo Dollar. The irony is that, in the future, these children are less likely to line up quietly than they were to begin with!

So, the question becomes, If I'm not going to use Dingo Dollars anymore, how do I get the children to do what I'm asking them to do? This is a topic that we are going to go more in-depth on in later chapters, but I'll give you a starting place now. You simply ask the children to do what you want them to do. There are a few ways to tweak requests that will maximize the chance that children will comply while still internalizing the rules we're trying to teach them. Collectively, researchers call these strategies *autonomy-supportive teaching*. Each of the strategies works by increasing students' feelings of autonomy while moving them closer to intrinsic motivation along the continuum we discussed earlier.

AUTONOMY-SUPPORTIVE TEACHING

Autonomy-supportive teaching involves four key actions:

- Recognizing children's feelings and perspectives
- Offering choices and encouraging initiative
- Minimizing controlling techniques that rely on external rewards or pressures
- Providing reasons for your requests whenever you can

First, recognize children's feelings and perspectives. When doing this, it helps to take a moment to think like a child. Not all children's actions make sense to us, but they generally make sense to their authors. We begin by understanding the perspectives of the children we are trying to motivate. By doing this, we are better able to align our requests with what will motivate them to comply. This approach lies at the heart of more extensive interventions such as functional behavior analysis* but is just as powerful as something that teachers can use all the time in smaller doses.

Next, we want to offer choices and encourage initiative. The goal is to balance the autonomy we give children against structures and limitations. For example, during independent reading time, we set up the structure that each child will be reading. We provide autonomy by letting them select the books. Always, we want to be mindful to provide children with as much autonomy as possible while still moving our classroom toward achieving our collective goals. Different activities and different groups of children will require different balances of autonomy and structure to maintain a healthy learning environment, but both ingredients should always be on your mind when you're creating and implementing your procedures and lessons. Again, by offering children meaningful choices, we give them opportunities to feel like they are in control of their own lives and learning, maximizing their motivation and engagement.**

Third, minimize controlling techniques that rely on external rewards or pressures. Using these will gain compliance in the short term but make our lives more difficult in the long term. To the degree that we can avoid bringing children down to the bottom

---

* Functional behavior analysis is an intensive process that involves more fully understanding not only the form (what a behavior looks like) but also a behavior's function (what it is helping the child obtain or avoid). It is generally used in formulating tier II and III interventions, so we will not delve into it too much here.

** This idea of balancing autonomy and control is one that we will come back to later in the book, so I will encourage you to continue thinking about it, as it is important.

of the motivation continuum, we should always strive to do so. As we've discussed, there are often hidden costs in using rewards and punishments in the classroom. Our brains struggle to balance multiple different kinds of motivation for doing something. When we begin offering rewards and punishments as a means to motivate children, we begin paving over any existing motivations. That's problematic, because young children especially are often already intrinsically motivated to behave.

To be clear, they often do not have the *ability* to behave, but they do have the motivation. From ages three to eight, children make huge gains in executive functioning, which includes the abilities to control where we place our attention, to balance our priorities, and to inhibit behaviors that we know we should not do. So we can expect that children's ability to behave will develop over the course of their time with us. Unfortunately, even as their ability develops, many teachers rob them of their motivation, meaning that teachers see challenging behavior grow over the course of the year rather than diminish.

Instead of thinking of rewards and punishments as baseline practices, good for the whole class, I like to think of external rewards and pressures as higher-level interventions, reserved for desperate occasions or for children who don't respond to the other techniques we're going to discuss.* There's nothing wrong with using rewards and punishments *after* I have explored other options, but they shouldn't be my default. When I do turn to them, I always keep an eye on how I am going to step down the intervention so that these children can eventually learn to self-regulate their behavior rather than relying on my controlling techniques. That way, I ensure that I am only bearing the downsides of rewards and punishments when the gain is worth more than the costs.

The final technique is probably my favorite. It's easy to use, intuitive, and incredibly powerful. Simply put, you should provide reasons for your requests whenever you can. There is something basic in the hardwiring of the human brain that looks for reasons to comply with requests. This makes *because* something of a magic word for us. A clever experiment conducted in the late '70s illustrates this nicely.

In 1978, Ellen Langer of Harvard University and two of her colleagues at the City University of New York, Arthur Blank and Benzion Chanowitz, designed an experiment to examine how people make decisions about doing favors for others. In this case, the favor involved letting a graduate student cut in line at the library copier. Keep in mind

---

* Some of you might recognize this sort of thinking from systems such as the Pyramid Model and Multi-Tiered Systems of Support.

that, back in the 1970s, copiers were not as plentiful as they are today, and there was no way to look up articles on the internet. If you wanted to read a chapter or a journal article back in your dorm room, you needed to use one of the two copiers that the library had.

The experimenters would wait for a line to form at the copier and then have the graduate student approach someone at the front of the line and ask to cut them. They systematically changed the way the graduate student phrased the request. Sometimes, the graduate student would simply say, "Excuse me, I have five pages. May I use the Xerox machine?" The favor in this case is small, so 60 percent of those approached allowed the graduate student to cut in line. Another group of times, the graduate student would say, "Excuse me, I have five pages. May I use the Xerox machine, because I'm in a rush?" We've all been there: running a few minutes behind and desperately trying to make a few copies before sprinting to a meeting or class where they will be distributed.* Unsurprisingly, a significantly greater number of people (94 percent) allowed the graduate student to cut in line when provided with this reason (Langer, Blank, and Chanowitz, 1978).

None of this should feel surprising. Many of us would reject the graduate student just asking to cut in line and would help the graduate student who made it clear that they were running late. The surprising result stems from the third group of times the graduate student would attempt to cut in line. In this scenario, the graduate student would say, "Excuse me, I have five pages. May I use the Xerox machine, because I have to make copies?" Why else would anyone be at a copier?! The researchers wanted (and succeeded) in creating a reason that was as asinine and meaningless as possible. What *is* surprising about this experiment is that 93 percent of the suckers thus approached allowed the graduate student to cut in line.

What do we take from this? Well, for starters, we don't begin supplying children with asinine, meaningless reasons to do the things we ask them to do. My personal least-favorite meaningless reason is "because I said so." We have all said these four words at some point because children can sometimes wear through our patience, but this is still a meaningless reason. These days, whenever I hear these words escape my lips, I immediately reflect on my request. Am I saying "because I said so" because my brain did not retrieve a good reason quickly enough? Or do I just not have a good reason for the behavior I'm asking of the children? When it's the former, I try to supply the real reason, even if it's tardy. When it's the latter, I reconsider the behavior and attempt to

---

* If your copy gods are anything like my copy gods, this is the point where paper jams will inevitably occur.

find an alternative behavior that will still meet my needs while allowing the children more autonomy.

What this study highlights for me is the importance of giving reasons for our requests. When we say the word *because*, we are inviting the receivers of our requests to internalize the reason and get behind what we are asking. As I discussed earlier, this kind of internalization is particularly important for children as this is, at its heart, how we socialize our children and prepare them to be productive members of a democratic society. Over time, when children internalize our requests, they are able to align their motivation with their burgeoning self-regulation abilities, thereby engaging in the kinds of behaviors that help them be successful on their own without the need for any adult regulation.

* * *

So, after three chapters of problematizing behaviorism, where does this leave us? I hope that I have conveyed the message that behaviorism is, at least, slightly problematic for us to use in the classroom on a daily basis. What I hope I am *not* conveying is that teachers should never use behaviorism. Rather, I am suggesting that behaviorism has specific uses where the benefits might outweigh the costs. Using a tiered support framework in which all children receive supports at the base of the pyramid to help them succeed, either academically or behaviorally, and fewer children need higher levels of support as we go up the pyramid, I generally place behaviorism at levels two and three. Thinking about our discussion of scaffolding, that support is incredibly useful for getting some children's feet onto the bottom rung of the ladder. Additionally, children with certain neurodivergences may fulfill their basic needs in different ways than other children. For them, rewards in particular may be integral in helping them connect with others and learn to self-regulate. Again, this raises the question of what we *should do*, which brings us to the next chapter.

CHAPTER 4: YOUR BRAIN IN THREE PARTS

Motivation and Frameworks

I think a good movie would be about a guy who's a brain scientist, but he gets hit on the head and it damages the part of the brain that makes you want to study the brain.

—JACK HANDEY,
AMERICAN HUMORIST

I first learned that behaviorism might be problematic while I was teaching kindergarten. I attended a professional development session provided by my school district's early childhood resource center. Up until that point, I had been using my trusty card chart and star chart to motivate my students to behave in the classroom. In one afternoon, the other kindergarten teachers at my school and I learned that we were not engaging in best practices. To say it was eye-opening would be an understatement. I distinctly remember the ride from the off-site training location back to school, with the five of us crammed into a small Ford Fusion. We all agreed during the car ride that the first order of business when we began school the next day would be to throw our antiquated card charts in the garbage and start doing things the right way.

I affectionately refer to the rest of that school year as my *Lord of the Flies* year.* True to my promise, I tossed out the card chart right in front of the children the very next day and announced that we were free from the cruel rule of the chart. My students, sensing the appropriate mood, cheered. The big problem here was that I had learned what not to do at that fateful seminar, but the details of what to replace my card chart with were a bit thin on the ground. To make matters worse, I had somehow confused *how* I motivated the children to do the right thing with whether or not I even should. The result was a sort of laissez-faire, hands-off approach to classroom management, where I allowed the children to do what they wanted as long as no one was in serious danger.

I lost a lot of hair that year. I was constantly frustrated by wanting the children to do one thing but being unsure of how to get them to do it without resorting to carrots or sticks.** Looking back on this, the sad thing is that I surely had the skill set to accomplish what I wanted when I began teaching, but relying on the crutch of behaviorism for so many years had caused those skills to atrophy and vanish.

In the interest of keeping you, dear reader, from making the same mistakes that I did, this chapter will be about what ended up replacing my laissez-faire system. Theory-wise, we will use self-determination theory, which we have already discussed, plus a heuristic of my own devising, and some basic underpinnings of neuroscience to support a classroom management system that maximizes children's motivation while simultaneously allowing teachers to set clear, consistent boundaries that promote

---

* Not just because of the pig's head that appeared on a stick outside my room one day but because of the utter lack of control I had over my class.

** Take a note here: Much of our frustration in the classroom stems not from children's behavior but from the size of the gap between children's behavior and our expectations.

positive child behaviors. In doing so, we will set children up for current and future success by promoting self-regulation and positive engagement in the classroom.

First, I want to remind you of something before we begin. Nothing is more effective than behaviorism in the short term at gaining compliance. I say this so that everyone goes into this with clear expectations. The system that we are going to discuss is at a disadvantage on day one. My opinion, however, is that the long-term benefits of this system will outweigh the short-term costs. That is to say, on day 180 in a behaviorist system, teachers tend to be dealing with the same behaviors they were dealing with on day one in exactly the same way—by passing out increasingly less effective carrots. As the year wears on, a behaviorist system gets more and more difficult to implement well. In our system, we will need to put in more effort at the beginning, when we won't have the supports of carrots and sticks, so that by day 180, the classroom will be running mostly on its own.

MOTIVATION + ABILITY = BEHAVIOR

Three key pieces dictate whether (or to what degree) a child will engage in a specific behavior. The figure below shows how I conceptualize these three pieces fitting together.

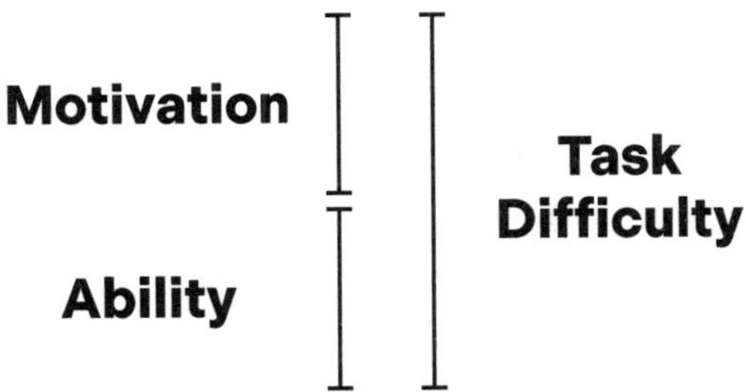

It shows the results of an equation that goes something like this:

Motivation + Ability = Behavior

We can compare the sum of motivation and ability to the difficulty of a task to understand the results we see when children try to engage in the task. When the sum of motivation and ability is greater than or equal to the difficulty of the task, children will be able to accomplish it. However, if children's motivation is diminished, even with the same ability level, children will not accomplish the task.

When I was teaching kindergarten, for example, I had a student in my class who was often wild during group time. He had trouble sitting still for even two or three minutes at a time and would frequently call out, move around, and distract other children. I tried numerous interventions to no avail. At some point, I concluded that he simply *couldn't* sit still for very long. Imagine my surprise about a month into the school year, when I watched him on the playground. He was playing a game with a group of other children and was assigned by the ringleader to play the role of a zombie. He was to lie there "dead" until someone came near him, at which point he was to jump up and chase the unfortunate victim. I watched, fascinated, as a minute ticked by with no one coming near him. Two minutes passed. Three. Four. Finally, after nearly five minutes of him lying there, completely motionless, one of the children trod near him. Up he popped, and off they went screaming as he chased the soul who had made the mistake of walking on his grave. I remember this so clearly, because the whole thing left me on the verge of tears. I had been struggling for a month to get even three minutes of silent stillness from him to no avail; yet here he was, exhibiting exactly that behavior when it benefited me not at all. I took important lessons from this: Play can be an incredible motivator, and many of the shortcomings we ascribe to children's lack of ability are, in fact, caused by a lack of motivation.

Conversely, there are times when children are as motivated as they can possibly be but simply don't have the ability to do something. The same year as the zombie incident, I had a Spanish-speaking student, Alessandra, in my class. In the classroom, I made a number of modifications to maximize her exposure to meaningful English and to allow her to function, including speaking more slowly, using visual cues, and figuring out how to say words in Spanish when necessary. In PE class, no such modifications were in place. I realized this when, two months into the school year, I received a note that the PE teacher sent me to forward on to Alessandra's mother, admonishing her student for not following directions. I had to sit down with the PE teacher and explain the situation. In fact, Alessandra was a phenomenal student and would have loved to follow the PE teacher's directions. However, no matter how strong her motivation was, her English ability would not allow her to do so without modifications. Using our previous model as an example, Alessandra's situation may have looked something like this:

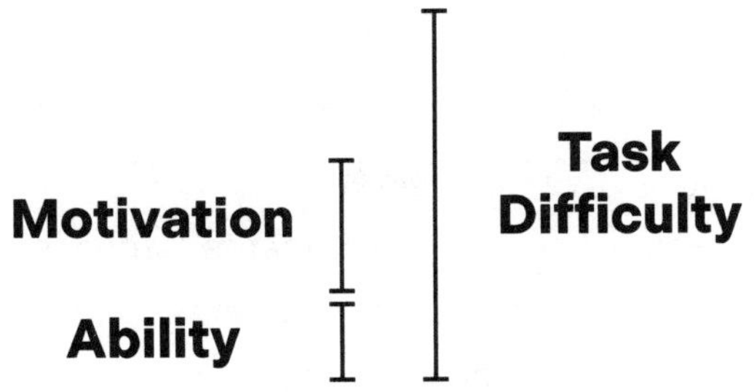

Motivation
Ability
Task Difficulty

Using this model, I hope you can see that there are three levers teachers can pull to influence student behavior.

- We can increase students' motivation.
- We can increase students' abilities.
- We can change the difficulty of the tasks.

I say *change* rather than *increase* or *decrease* because the direction we move depends on the nature of the task or behavior. If I have a student who is hitting other students with blocks, I want to make that task more difficult. On the other hand, if a student is having difficulty sitting quietly in whole group, I want to make that task easier. This three-lever system provides the basis for my thoughts on how to manage behavior. Everything we build around it will simply be to enhance the effectiveness of these three levers. In this chapter, we will begin discussing the motivation piece of the model.

I spoke earlier of the costs and benefits of behaviorism with respect to motivation. Using our little three-lever model, we can see that on day one of the school year, reward-based motivation from behaviorism gives us the most bang for our buck. As the year goes on, it decreases in effectiveness, decreasing the motivation of students without altering ability or task difficulty. Moreover, as you will remember from previous chapters, it diminishes other sources of motivation as well. This is why, even though it is tempting to start the year with behaviorism and then transfer to another type of motivation, we should resist doing so unless there is no other way. Rather, we will start the year with less motivation and quickly build up motivation in a fashion that will serve the children and us in the long term by fulfilling their needs for autonomy, relatedness, and competence.

FULFILLING CHILDREN'S NEED FOR RELATEDNESS WITH US

I want to begin our discussion with fulfilling students' needs for relatedness. The basic desire for relatedness is one of attachment and connection. The fastest way to build such attachment and connection is through unconditional love. Even as I type that, I worry that it's too hokey, but it is, without a doubt, what forms the foundation of all strong relationships.

I also want to clarify that when I say to love unconditionally, I am not talking about a feeling. If I love my wife but treat her consistently with scorn, condescension, and disdain, I will not fulfill her need for relatedness. In the context of the classroom (and, I would argue, in settings beyond the scope of this book), what really matters is how we treat others. As Saint Thérèse put it so succinctly, "It isn't enough to love; we must prove it."

This is the opposite of using rewards and punishments to control how children act in the classroom. By definition, rewards and punishments are conditional. *If* you do this, *then* you can have that. I have heard far too many children suggest that their teacher does not love them when they move their clip, flip their card, or send a note home to believe that children interpret this conditional behavior on the part of the teacher as anything other than a sign of conditional regard and affection.

The opposite of this is to treat all children positively, regardless of their behavior. To illustrate, I want to talk about a practice I used to implement in my own classroom called Fun Friday. In my first-grade classroom, children who kept their card on the top color (yellow) for the entire week and moved their stars up at least one day got to attend Fun Friday. Fun Friday was always amazing. In the summer, we had popsicles outside or played kickball. In the winter, we bundled up to watch Reading Rainbow and drink hot chocolate. Predictably, the same children did not get to attend Fun Friday nearly every week (reminding us that sometimes, a lack of a positive reward effectively functions like a punishment). These four or five forlorn boys would have to stay in the classroom with my teaching assistant, working on their penmanship or some other tedious task, while the rest of the children enjoyed their final hour in school each week. Looking back, I have no doubt in my mind that this hour each week served only to emphasize to these boys that school was not a place for them, that they didn't belong, and that I personally didn't like them. To be blunt, I was simultaneously frustrating all three of their needs (autonomy, relatedness, and competence), thus lowering their motivation week after week after week. It is no wonder they rose up against me. In the end, it didn't matter how I felt about the boys who weren't going to Fun Friday. I could have loved them and cared for them in my heart, but every week I was *showing* them that I didn't love or care for them by my actions.

After fixing my classroom management practices, I kept Fun Friday (more on that in chapter 5). The difference was that all children attended, regardless of what happened during the week. I don't want to spoil chapter 5 for you, but the result was a group of children who *all* knew that I loved them and cared for them and wanted them to be happy.

HELPING CHILDREN FEEL SAFE

Fun Friday for All is a nice example of a routine in the classroom that can set us up for success or failure. Ahead of time, I thought out what I wanted to do and then did it. These are probably the easiest things to change out of all our practices. Greeting every child warmly when they walk through the door is something we all just have to decide we're doing and then do it. Therefore, it's worth spending some significant time reflecting on our daily schedule and practices to ensure that we are doing it right. Moreover, these practices and routines should start on day one and continue throughout the year. One of my key goals in building a strong relationship with the children was for all of them to know that they were safe, physically and psychologically. Safety may feel like an odd goal to have in a classroom, but neuroscience suggests that it's an incredibly important one.

To vastly oversimplify an incredibly complex conceptual model, our brains can be roughly divided into three parts: the brain stem, the limbic system, and the neocortex. The neocortex controls most of our higher functions, such as cognition, language, reasoning, and sensory perception. The limbic system handles functions such as emotion, motivation, and long-term memory. Our brain stems, on the other hand, control many of the automatic functions of our bodies. They keep our hearts beating and our lungs pumping. We don't have to think about these things for them to occur. They just do. There is also a structure in the brain stem (the *locus coeruleus* for those of you who are giant nerds) that regulates our responses to pain, panic, and stress. When we experience acute stress or panic (such as being in a car accident or hearing a nearby gunshot), this node causes adrenaline and noradrenaline to be released into our bloodstreams. These chemicals allow us to become more alert, stronger, and faster. This is an incredibly important system to be able to take advantage of if there is an actual emergency. Unfortunately, one of the side effects of the system is that it inhibits functions in other parts of the brain. Because it is rare that we need to solve complex math problems while experiencing an emergency, our brains allocate resources accordingly, shutting down the neocortex with a flood of dopamine so we can focus on survival.

Most teachers are adults from middle- or upper-class backgrounds. As such, we are largely in control of our own lives. Threats to our safety are rare. Our brains have spent years regulating themselves in an environment of safety. Unfortunately, for many of the children in our classrooms, especially those who exhibit challenging behaviors, their brains have not had that luxury. One of the unfortunate things about the locus coeruleus is that, like many areas in the brain, the more it's activated, the easier it is to activate. That is, it may take something surprising or painful or scary to activate it the first time, but something less surprising or painful or scary will activate it the second time. Over time, it becomes activated more and more readily. By the time children show up in a kindergarten classroom, something as benign as a teacher yelling at another student about spilling paint can activate this part of the brain. For some children, this can lead to a response where the student freezes. For others, it can lead to a response where the child becomes aggressive. What it *never* leads to is a situation where the child learns easily and is responsive to thinking and reasoning.

Because of this, I define *safety* broadly in the classroom. It's not just about feeling physically safe, although that is important. It's about feeling emotionally and psychologically safe as well. Children need to know that, no matter what is going on in the rest of their lives, the classroom is a place where they can be warm and safe and loved and cared for. Classrooms should be places of joy and wonder, something that's easy to forget in the rush of standards and assessments and pedagogy. The irony is that when we push to handle these other things and lose the joy and wonder, we create stressful spaces that prevent many children from learning at all because their brains won't let them. It's not enough to create a warm, safe, loving space on day one and assume that's that. We must then walk the walk for the rest of the year.

On the first day of each school year, I would sit down with the children and talk about how the year will be a challenging one and the only way we will get through it is together (more on this in the next chapter). As soon as I finished my talk about supporting one another, I would turn to how we embody that in the classroom. I would explain to the children that I have two jobs in the classroom. My first job is to make sure everyone has safe bodies and happy hearts. My second job is to make sure that every child in the classroom learns what they need to learn. If you are a child in my classroom, you have one job, which is to help me with my two jobs.*

I love this framework because it is simple and elegant, and any issue that arises in the classroom can be dealt with using the two jobs. I want to be sure to define what I mean by each element so we're all on the same page. When I say *safe bodies*, I don't mean that I'm trying to protect children from every bump or scratch. An important part of developing self-regulation is experiencing consequences that come from a failure to self-regulate. If I other-regulated the children every moment of the day, they would never experience those consequences and never learn. What I do want to accomplish is preventing any grievous bodily harm or any situations where the actions of one child lead to hurting another.

Similarly, *happy hearts* doesn't mean every child is happy every moment of the day. In every classroom on nearly every day, there are times when children become unhappy. Some nights, when you're a kindergartener, you fall asleep and dream. In these dreams, the Lord on high, seated among all the angels and the choir of the heavenly hosts, speaks with the kindergartener. He says, "Whom shall I send to be line leader, and who will go forth to lead the class to the cafeteria?" The kindergartener responds, "Here am I. Send me," but when they awake and go to school, stupid dumb Zoe's name is next to the line-leader icon on the job board, and even though this poor kindergartener attempts to explain the divine right by which they should be the line leader, the stupid dumb teacher won't let them, and they know that they will never be happy again!

It's okay for children to feel sad or angry, and my job is not to get them back to feeling happy as quickly as possible. My job is to teach them to acknowledge and understand their feelings so they can regulate themselves, no matter how they feel. So instead, when I say "happy hearts," I'm referring to what I brought up earlier: that children come to my classroom every day and feel like it is a safe place where they are loved and cared for no matter what, and that it is filled with joy and wonder. That sort of environment puts their brains in the right state, so they have the best chance to succeed, no matter what their feelings are at any one moment.

A frequent question that teachers have for me when they begin thinking critically about motivation and how we fulfill children's need for relatedness arises from the role of consequences. That is, if I am not using the Think About What You've Done

* Like all good ideas in teaching, I shamelessly stole this one. I originally saw it in my mentor Kim Hughes's classroom. As I mentioned in the introduction, she is a former North Carolina Teacher of the Year and remains one of the most amazing educators I have ever known.

With Your Life Chair™ or stickers or treasure boxes to motivate children, does that mean there are no consequences for when they do things they shouldn't do? There are indeed consequences. However, the purpose of the consequences is not to serve as rewards or punishments to shape children's behavior. Instead, consequences flow from my two jobs. If a child is doing something that prevents those things, I will do what it takes to do my jobs in a way that infringes on a child's needs as little as possible.

There are two key points I want to be clear about here. First, doing your jobs takes precedence over everything else. You have to keep children physically and psychologically safe. Even if you have to infringe on a child's need for autonomy to do it, you should do it. Second, you should always impose consequences sequentially so that you move from those that infringe the least on a child's ability to fulfill their needs to those that more heavily infringe on a child's ability to fulfill their needs.

For example, if a child is "hunting dinosaurs" in the blocks center by throwing wooden blocks at other children, you will have to stop them from doing so. I usually start with a verbal explanation of how the behavior is preventing me from doing my jobs and how they can use the blocks safely. This approach infringes very little on my hunter's ability to fulfill their need for autonomy. However, if I turn around a few minutes later and blocks are once again flying, I will need to find a consequence that goes further to prevent the child from hurting another. In this case, I might ask them to choose a different center for the rest of that day's center time, letting them know that they can return to the blocks center tomorrow. I will also expand on my previous explanation as to why I am having to limit their choices. To reiterate, the point here is not to punish them for throwing blocks so they are less likely to throw blocks in the future. It's to keep everyone safe *now*.

If they return the next day and throw blocks again, I will ask them to remain away from blocks until I give them permission to return. I will pair this with teaching them appropriate blocks behavior, which we will cover in chapter 8. As the child learns the skills they need to be successful in blocks, I will reintroduce them to blocks with scaffolds in place to support their new skills. First, I might go into blocks with them. Then, I might put them with a single partner with whom I know they work well. Then, I might introduce a third, specifically chosen partner. Finally, I will let them go for small amounts of time to the center when they wish until they arrive back at a level of full autonomy, going to blocks when they choose, with whom they choose, for as long as they choose.

THE MAGIC RATIO

John Gottman is a researcher who specializes in relationships. In his earlier years, he focused largely on marriage and using science to understand what makes for a successful marriage. His team's research and analysis on the topic have probably done more than anyone else's to shine a light on exactly what makes marriages work and what leads to their demise. For many years, his claim to fame was that he could watch a fifteen-minute video of a couple discussing something on which they disagreed (not having an argument or fight, per se, just a discussion) and with over 90 percent accuracy, predict which couples would be divorced within five years (Gottman, 1991). Mind-blowing stuff.

One interesting little finding from Gottman's work that has moved from his research into the public consciousness is the "magic ratio." The magic ratio describes how many positive interactions a healthy couple should have to balance out each negative interaction. It turns out that couples who have five positive interactions for each negative interaction are much more likely to stay happily together than those with fewer positive interactions.

After learning this, I first began looking at my own interactions with my wife, but almost immediately after that, I started to wonder about classrooms. I would go in and observe teachers for a variety of reasons, but I started just keeping some side notes for myself, looking at how many positive interactions teachers were having with children for each negative interaction. I was surprised at how well the ratio held up for teachers and students. When I saw teachers having five or more positive interactions with children for each negative one, they seemed strongly connected. When the ratio leaned the other way, anger and resentment seemed to build. Now, when I do coaching and consultation, this ratio is one of the first things I look at.

INCREASING POSITIVE INTERACTIONS

Over my years of working with teachers, I have found that there are two ways to approach the magic ratio in the classroom. The first is to increase the number of positive interactions. This is where I went first, and I will tell you that it is difficult but possible and important to do. Just as we intentionally think about what we will teach during our small-group time or during our morning whole group, we must start thinking about how we build and maintain relationships with individual children.

Gottman's team lists eight ways that couples can have positive interactions:

- being interested in the other person,
- expressing affection,
- demonstrating that they matter,
- intentionally appreciating something about the other person,
- finding opportunities for agreement,
- empathizing and apologizing when you make a mistake,
- accepting the other person's perspective, and
- joking or playing with the other individual (Benson, 2017).

Obviously, each of these ways looks different in a classroom relationship than in a marriage, but I have found each to be a powerful way to build rapport with children.

I don't think anyone needs to do this for a long period of time, but it's eye-opening to track these behaviors over the course of a week. Teachers are often shocked to find that they invest quite a bit of time and effort in building relationships with particular children while others only receive group-directed or teaching attention. Working with children to teach them a skill, piece of knowledge, or behavior is different than having the sorts of personal, positive interactions Gottman advocates for. If you sit down and make a list of the children as they come to mind, you will probably list your best- and worst-behaved students first. Quieter children often come at the end of the list. Frequently, these children would benefit from a little more positive attention as much as the children who exhibit challenging behaviors.

Instead of just assuming that positive interactions will occur because you are occupying shared space, it is worth making specific times in your schedule dedicated to nothing more than building relationships through positive interactions. That might mean simply playing with children and talking about their weekends during Monday's arrival time. It might mean taking the time to have lunch with a small group of children each week and sharing with them what you appreciate about them. It could mean standing by the door as children leave to let them know how much you will miss them and care about them. There is no one right way to do this, and you will want to play to your own strengths and abilities. What really matters, in my experience, is that these times reside in your daily schedule and happen with some frequency and that you are intentional about having these positive interactions rather than leaving them to chance or fate.

REDUCING NEGATIVE INTERACTIONS

The other side of the coin, of course, is reducing negative interactions. I find this strategy to be particularly important, as it is difficult to achieve the magic ratio if you are regularly having negative interactions with children. Think about it: five positive interactions with each child after you yell at the class will take forever.* Being intentional about positive interactions is fairly simple and straightforward—you just have to go have more positive interactions. Being intentional about reducing negative interactions is far more difficult.

Negative interactions often arise from parts of our brain over which we have less conscious control. Something happens in our class to upset us, our cortisol levels rise, our brains turn off our prefrontal cortex, and our limbic system causes us to say or do something that we may regret later. How do we stop this from occurring when a hallmark of the process is that it involves a non-conscious part of our brains?

Fortunately for us, our brains have evolved with a mechanism for just this occasion. We have feedback loops built into our brain's architecture that run from our limbic system to our prefrontal cortex and back. This feedback loop is what keeps us from turning into the Incredible Hulk and just staying that way forever. When our limbic system is activated strongly, our brain essentially runs periodic checks where it briefly turns on our prefrontal cortex and asks, "Is it time to calm down yet?" If the answer is yes, our brain starts to shift resources from the limbic system back to the prefrontal cortex. If the answer is no, the brain continues in its current state. For children, this feedback loop barely works. There are physiological processes that begin around age four or five (and are not fully complete until our twenties) that make this feedback loop more effective. Because of this, children have much more trouble than we do regulating their emotions.

As many of you reading this will recognize, we still run into plenty of opportunities to lose our cool. In *Conscious Discipline*, Becky Bailey (2015) talks about not giving control of our emotions to children. That is, we should remain in control of how we feel rather than letting children dictate how we feel. Sometimes, this is possible. If we are focused on emotional regulation the entire time we are teaching, we can remain fully in control. However, as we will discuss later in this book, much of our brain's activity runs on habit and autopilot, leaving us open to emotional dysregulation that can be difficult or impossible to prevent.

---

* Ain't nobody got time for that!

So many teachers with whom I work know they should remain calm in the face of challenging behavior yet consistently fail to do so when they are on the receiving end of spit or a thrown chair. This is totally understandable. Our brains have evolved to react quickly and unthinkingly when we are threatened. This sort of thing keeps you alive when you are being chased by a lion but can cause overreaction when you are being chased by a five-year-old child.

A basic tenet of neuroscience is that our brain is filled with pathways and connections. These pathways and connections are what allow us to have particular ideas and make connections between things. They allow us to do particular actions with our bodies and execute specific skills and behaviors. The pathways that support what we do repeatedly are strengthened over time, while those that we never use tend to be pruned. The strengthening of some pathways and removal of others allows our brains to operate in the most efficient manner possible. Therefore, to take control and stop ourselves from overreacting, we will need to strengthen our brains' feedback loops. That is, we will need to practice the skill of emotional regulation to get better at it.

I used to feel the way to do this was to take more conscious control of my brain's emotional state and not let children dictate how I felt. I found that this worked well when I only needed to regulate for a short amount of time. For example, if I walk into a classroom for an hour to help a teacher with a child's challenging behavior, I can decide before I walk in how I will feel and react. Since I only need to keep this up for an hour, it is doable. However, when my own child is exhibiting challenging behavior, maintaining conscious control of my emotions is more difficult. He has an uncanny knack for choosing times when I am tired or distracted to really let me have it, and in those times, I am vulnerable to my brain's automatic processes.

Knowing that we cannot always practice this skill of emotional regulation in our classrooms, we need to find a way to do so outside the classroom. I often think of this in terms of sports. When I played soccer in my youth, we would dribble balls between cones, shoot over and over again at the goal, and play keep-away games with a circle of people on the outside keeping the ball from two people on the inside. These activities are not the game, but they strengthened the abilities we would use in the game. It's the same here. We will do something that reinforces and strengthens our feedback loop so that when we need it in the classroom, it will be more easily activated.

I sometimes meet resistance from teachers who believe that our emotional regulation is something we are born with and not something we can cultivate. We will talk more about this belief in chapter 7, but for now, if you have doubts, let's do a brief exercise to illustrate how plastic and changeable the brain is. In a moment, I want you to put the book down. I want you to point straight ahead with the aptly named pointer finger on your left hand. Keep your thumb down to make sure you're not making a finger gun. With your right hand, do a thumbs-up. Now, switch so your left hand is doing a thumbs-up and your right hand is pointing straight ahead. Then, switch back. Right here is where you stop reading and do the things. Go ahead. I'll still be here when you get back. Did you do it? If the answer is no, what are you still reading for? Put the book down.

Okay, if you are like 98 percent of the people with whom I work, this was more difficult than you thought it would be. You probably had a moment when you thought, "Why am I doing this?" Then, when you tried to do it, you had a moment of panic when you worried that your body was no longer under your brain's control. Doing this movement is difficult because the pathways in your brain that control these simultaneous movements are weak. However, I want you to spend five minutes just slowly switching back and forth. That is, I want you to practice this useless skill for five minutes.

At the end of the five minutes, I suspect you will find a pronounced difference between how you are currently doing at switching your fingers versus how you did the first time. The reason is that each time you do the switch, the connections between the neurons in your brain that govern those movements become stronger. We will be using this same approach to practice the technique that allows us to prevent negative interactions in the classroom.

LET IT GO

Before we get to the technique itself, I hope you'll indulge me in one more aside. (This one doesn't involve me tricking you into worrying that you don't know how to use your hands.) In my ninth-grade social studies class, we learned about Siddhartha Gautama, commonly known as the Buddha. As the story goes, Siddhartha begins life as the son of a wealthy man raised in a palace in India. He is isolated in his palace, wanting for nothing. One day, at age twenty-nine, he decides to leave his home and go out into the city. There, he sees an old man, a diseased man, a decaying corpse, and an ascetic. The first three show Siddhartha that suffering is inevitable in this world. The fourth shows him a path to relinquish fear of that suffering. He then goes to sit under a bodhi tree to meditate. While meditating, he reaches enlightenment, spending the rest of his life guiding others toward this state of perfect being. His teachings centered on letting go of all desires and wants, for in doing so, one would have nothing that could be taken from them by death or disease or suffering.

As a fourteen-year-old, all of this sounded mystical to me. I remember seeing pictures in my textbook of people sitting in half- or full-lotus position, their eyes closed and a sublime expression on their faces. However, the central message the Buddha was delivering—that all life is suffering—seemed clearly negative. I struggled to make the connection between meditating to let go of all the bad (and good) things in my life and being happy.

Fast-forward to 2020, and the world is a burning dumpster fire. We're all trapped inside* due to COVID. Zoom meetings were actually enjoyable because at least they allowed us to connect to someone outside our immediate household. (You know that things have gone awry if a Zoom meeting is the high point of your day.) I found myself, as did many others, filled with anxiety and ennui. In trying to address my negative emotions, I did what I imagine any of us would do: I started reading peer-reviewed journal articles.**

I was surprised to find that, between my time in ninth grade and 2020, meditation had become a widely studied practice in the West. Countless journal articles attested to the benefits of meditation, or *mindfulness*, as it is often called. I remained unclear as to why mindfulness worked or even what exactly it was supposed to help with, but I decided to start practicing it. I downloaded an app, and each day for fifteen minutes, I would close my eyes and follow the directions of the voice from my phone. It would take me three years of meditation and study before I finally began to understand what mindfulness was doing for me.

To fully explore what mindfulness is doing to our brains and thoughts is beyond the scope of this chapter. However, I will zoom in on one particular change that occurs through the practice. When I meditate, I focus on my breathing. At first, I thought that the lesson for my brain in this was focus. I suspected that I was training my brain to place its attention on one thing to the exclusion of all others. Therefore, at the beginning of my practice, I would grab my attention with an iron will and hold it desperately on the in and out of my chest and diaphragm.

---

* Some of us with young children!

** Obviously, I'm kidding. If you find yourself reading peer-reviewed journal articles to solve personal problems, this is a surefire sign that you should be seeking professional help.

The voice from my phone, though, kept advising against this, so I knew that I was doing it wrong. I tried a lighter touch, but my ADHD brain would then spend much of the fifteen minutes bounding from place to place and thought to thought. Again, I knew that I was failing at meditation. Like many of you when you realized that you can't do something as simple as shift between pointing and giving a thumbs-up, I was dismayed at how bad I was at this skill, which was supposed to make my life immeasurably better.

Three years after beginning my journey, I finally grasped one of the key benefits of meditation. When we focus only on our breathing, thoughts and emotions will happen. This is the brain's natural function. Rather than fighting these thoughts or feelings and holding my attention elsewhere by iron will, and rather than giving these thoughts and feelings free rein to run from place to place, to be mindful is to recognize these thoughts and feelings as they arise and then to let them go, nonjudgmentally, without thinking or feeling any way about them. That is, I don't judge myself for thinking about things other than my breath. I don't get frustrated because these thoughts keep coming up. Rather, I label them and then let them go. Because my natural resting point is my breath, I don't even have to push them away. I just say to myself, "frustration," and then I let that feeling go and gently move back to my focus on the rise and fall of my chest, the feeling of air moving through my sinuses.

Meditation, it turns out, is not about what you are doing but rather what you aren't doing. When we meditate, we are training our brains to let go of feelings or extraneous thoughts. This is exactly the pathway in our brain that we want to strengthen. Having done this every day for three years, I am convinced that the research literature on mindfulness is correct. Among other advantages, meditating daily appears to provide us with an improved ability to let go of challenging thoughts and emotions, even when we are not meditating.

So how do we apply this skill in the classroom? When we are experiencing a challenging situation, it is likely that our cortisol level will rise and we will get angry, frustrated, or upset. This is natural, even if it isn't helpful. Meditation trains our brains to deal with this in the most effective way possible. When we feel angry, the best course of action is to notice the emotion, label it, and then let it go. For example, if I am in a classroom and a child spits in my face, I will absolutely get angry. I will feel my muscles tighten, my brow furrow, and my mouth turn down. Because I have practiced so often, however, my brain will notice these things. Then, I say to myself, "I'm feeling angry," and I let go of the emotion. This leaves me in a place to deal with the situation with a clear head, reducing the likelihood that I will say or do something that pours gasoline on the fire of an already tense moment. In doing so, I am preserving my relationship with the children and avoiding the common mistake of making a mountain out of a behavioral molehill.

* * *

This idea of fostering relationships brings me back to the teacher's own role. I talked about setting up a classroom community based on the idea of love as a demonstrated practice to build our relationships with children, but our responsibility doesn't end there. Indeed, this kind of classroom community provides the right environment for positive relationships to occur, so it would be foolish of us not to take advantage. In the next chapter, we will tackle the nuts and bolts of how we can take this foundation of fulfilling children's need for relatedness and crank it up to eleven by helping them fulfill their need for relatedness with one another.

CHAPTER 5: CLASSROOM COMMUNITY

Identity, Rituals, and Colonoscopies (Oh My!)

All the higher functions originate as actual relations between human individuals.

—LEV VYGOTSKY,
PSYCHOLOGIST

In chapter 4, we covered the basics of fulfilling children's need for relatedness, and we focused on our own relationship with children. Here, we will turn our attention to helping children fulfill their need for relatedness with one another. These are both key. When children's need for a positive relationship with us and their need to have a positive relationship with their peers is fulfilled, we are going to see fewer maladaptive behavioral patterns emerge. (If you're feeling too tired, rundown, and listless to turn back to chapter 2 to remind yourself what these are, *maladaptive behavioral pattern* is the fancy name psychologists give to behaviors that help us fulfill our needs in the short term but lead to long-term negative outcomes. And don't worry if you forgot about them altogether. Eventually, you'll have heard me yammer on about them enough that you'll find yourself casually dropping the term into party conversations, causing your once friends and acquaintances to slowly edge away from you in favor of someone who will stick to less sexy topics, such as the weather or Dan Quayle's *potatoe*).

What if we wanted to juice this classroom community thing, though? Doing so could yield benefits that go beyond those related to challenging behaviors. Building strong classroom communities has the potential to improve learning, attendance, and a host of other outcomes for us and for children. It turns out that organizational psychology, social psychology, and behavioral economics have plenty to teach us about how to form strong group bonds, influence how children view their time in our classroom, and build cohesion around the pursuit of shared goals. In this chapter, we will explore how some of these theories can help us create the classroom communities we've always dreamed of.

Each year, on the first day of the school year (or Move-Up Day, when I taught preschool), I would sit my class down, and I would promise them a little bit of honesty. I would say, "Listen, this year is going to be hard. We're going to have fun, but there are also going to be days when you get upset. There are going to be days where you're sad or frustrated or angry, or when you just feel really down. That's okay, though, because on those days, someone else in this room is going to lift you up. Kindergarten (or preschool) is a long, hard, difficult journey, and the only way we're going to get to the end of it is together."

I believe that. Many times, the person who was down was one of the children, but other times, it was me or my assistant. Once I started working within this framework, where I built a classroom community focused on everyone supporting everyone else, I never saw a situation that, as a group, we couldn't handle. As we move through the rest of the chapter together, this idea will serve as the foundation for everything else.

That is, everything else is in service to this goal of building a community that watches out for one another, that sees problems and turns toward the person having difficulty instead of away, and that moves forward with a shared vision.

GROUP IDENTITY

When I taught, I liked to have a specific identity for each of my classes. Having that identity was important and formed the core of "who we were" as a group. We will get to autonomy shortly, but for reasons that I hope are obvious by now, I allowed the children to choose that group identity each year. One year, I had a lot of girls in my class. That year, we were Mr. Holland's Ponies. (Spoiler alert for the autonomy chapter: sometimes giving children autonomy means that you won't get to do things the way you would have wanted.) This shared identity then formed the core of what we did on a day-to-day basis. Our room decor became aggressively horse-themed, including a barn-style book nook complete with hay. When I needed their attention, I would say, "Pony up!" and they would stand up, shake out their manes, and nicker. As soon as it was time for my class to go, I would click twice with my mouth. Walking outside to recess was generally done with an accompaniment—me, at the back of the line, banging two halves of a coconut together.*

The next year, much to my delight, my students voted for pirates, leading us to be Mr. Holland's Buccaneers.** My teaching assistant painted a giant pirate ship on the back windows of my room. Children who were working on something and did not wish to be disturbed could wear a pirate hat that would indicate this status. When I needed to get the children's attention, I would say, "One, two, three, eye on me," and my class would respond by putting a hand over one eye, like a patch, and saying, "Arrrrr!" in their best pirate voices. I would do my countdown in a pirate voice when it was time to leave the playground, and when I got to zero, the kids would all shout, "Shiver me timbers!" It was a lot of fun, but it was also *who we were*, and my students knew it.

Sometimes on the playground, children from other classes would come over while we were doing a fun pirate cheer or counting down, and they would say, "I want to be a pirate with you guys!" I would look those kids dead in the eye and say, "Absolutely not! Go back to Mrs. White." Whenever I tell groups this during professional development

---

* Props to the Foley artist on *Monty Python and the Holy Grail*, because I could never get mine to sound that good.

** Where does a pirate keep his buccaneers? Under his buckin' hat.

sessions, they always laugh, like I'm joking, but I need you to understand, I'm not joking. Social psychologists teach us that our group memberships are about who is in the group, but it is also about who is not in the group (Thibaut and Kelley, 1959). That is, groups have boundaries, and those boundaries are important because we tend to work better with individuals who are in our group versus out of our group. We tend to like members of our group better, believe they are better at their jobs, give them more favorable attributions, are more willing to share with them, provide more assistance to them, and support them when they are having a difficult time.

I never suggest that we do not like the other classes or that we are in competition with them. It is simply that we are a team. Like I said on day one, kindergarten is a long, hard, difficult journey, and the only way we get there is together. Being a buccaneer or a pony means you get to do the fun stuff, but it also means being there when someone is having a tough time. It means doing the cheers, but it also means lifting other ponies or buccaneers up when they fall. The children understand this, so they understand why we don't include everyone in the good parts when they aren't there for the hard parts. We each know one another's journey and the hardships, so we celebrate all the more during the good moments. This is what classroom community is. It is not just sharing space and breathing the same air. It's relying on one another and celebrating with one another in turn. When we help children cement their understanding of this, we reap benefits that go far beyond just improved motivation.

FOSTERING RELATEDNESS

Getting children to turn toward one another in tough times can require some extra help on occasion. In Becky Bailey's (2015) *Conscious Discipline*, one of the practices she advocates is the presence of a We Care Bag. I want to use this practice as an example of how we foster interpersonal trust and relationships between children. Every teacher uses the We Care Bag a little differently, but in my classroom, the We Care Bag hung on the wall near our cubbies. It contained a stuffed animal, a blanket, adhesive bandages, magic lotion (lotion with a little glitter in it, which cures most ailments), and a couple other assorted items that the children requested go in the bag. In short, the We Care Bag is used to help someone who is having a difficult time to feel better. The real trick of the We Care Bag is that neither my instructional assistant nor I ever touched it. Instead, we had a child get it down from the wall on the first week of school and unpack it during our whole-group time. Then, we talked about how any child in the class could get it to help someone who is having a difficult time, because we all have those.

As I'm sure you can imagine, left to their own devices, children would get the bag down at every inappropriate time and simply play with the goodies inside. To prevent this, we talked ad nauseam about how to identify when someone is having a difficult time, when it might not be appropriate to grab the bag, how to decide who takes it if multiple people think of using the bag, how to gracefully turn down the bag if you don't want it, how to handle it when someone doesn't want the bag but isn't turning it down gracefully, and so on and so forth. Then, throughout the year, we would bring the topic up and critique our uses of the bag to make sure we all remained on the same page. Over the course of the school year, these rehearsals and discussions and practices took many hours away from our precious instructional time.

Honestly, the bag is fine, but the point of the bag for me was never the bag itself. I would estimate its effectiveness at soothing children at a less than 50 percent success rate. So why were we happy to invest all those hours in its use? Because the bag is a tool that we use to reshape how children think of themselves and their role in the classroom. The use of the bag teaches children how to embody the idea that we only make it through the journey together. In Mr. Holland's class, your job is not to take care of yourself. Your job is to take care of everyone.

The pull of relational aggression is hard on five-year-olds. It's so tempting for them to laugh at someone who is freaking out because they need to get off the computer or to ignore and awkwardly side-eye someone who is crying because they were tagged in a game of Cross the Ocean. The bag is a tool that helps them overcome those five-year-old tendencies. It helps shape them into individuals who are caring and capable of fulfilling one another's need for relatedness. The bag is just one example of this. I encourage those of you who work in classrooms to think critically about this concept, because it's not enough for us to establish strong relationships with children. We have to help them establish strong relationships with one another. It's worth taking time to come up with your own ways of fostering relatedness between children so that they can take up this role of supporting others.

RITUALS AND ROUTINES

Setting the boundaries of where our group ends is important, but I also think it is important to set the boundaries of *when* our community begins and ends. Imagine you have a child who is sleeping soundly on a Monday morning. He got back from a trip late the night before, so he is tired. His mom runs into his room at 7:00 AM and yells, "Why aren't you up?! I have to be at work in thirty minutes!" She runs out, but he is so tired that he barely registers what she said. A few minutes later, she runs back in and yells, "I told you to get up! You're going to make me late!" She physically drags him out of bed and begins pulling his clothes off him. She points to the clothes she laid out for him the night before and yells, "Put those on! We have to go!" Still half-asleep, he pulls on his shirt, pants, socks, and shoes. His mom returns to pull him out of his bedroom, down the stairs, and out the front door.

"What about breakfast?" he asks. "We don't have time for breakfast," his mom replies, practically tossing him into the car in her haste. She drops him at his bus stop a couple of minutes later and then heads on to work. When your student gets on the bus, he is immediately ridiculed because he put his shirt on backwards. He punches one of the bullies, which causes the bus driver to stop the bus, yell at him, and bring him to the front of the bus. When they arrive at school, he is forced to endure another dressing down by the principal before he is allowed to come to your preschool classroom. Now, this hangry, sullen, seething young boy steps through your door.

This sort of thing happens daily in our classes. Stress and trauma do not respect the boundaries of classroom walls, so it is up to us to find ways to separate all that from what happens inside our spaces and in our communities. One way that we do this is through rituals and routines. Rituals and routines build group cohesion, foster our shared identity, and help us and the children clarify our shared goals and values. Here, I want to share the ritual I used to separate my classroom community from all the nonsense that happens to children in the morning. We cannot control what comes before, but we can control how we help children leave it behind, rather than expecting three-, four-, or five-year-olds to self-regulate at that level.

During my arrival time, I used to let my students play in free-choice centers. Doing so provided multiple benefits. Children think about the first thing they do when they arrive, and if it's fun, they'll look forward to it. I also had children who were desperate to play in a particular center, and having two free-choice center times, even in kindergarten, allowed them to find one time or the other to do what they wanted to do. Finally, this practice freed me up to greet and hug and assess and work with children one-on-one without having to lead a class-wide activity or spend too much time regulating behavior.

When the bell rang, I would put on the cleanup song. I like an upbeat cleanup song,* so as soon as the song came on, we would hit the ground running. The goal was always to tidy the room before the song was over. I'd be charging around the room like a field general, pointing and giving orders: "Charlie, put those vegetables in the dramatic play fridge!" or "The blocks center looks good. You all go help Axel hang those dresses up!" As we got close to finishing our cleaning, instead of sending children to help others, I would begin to send them to the back of the room, near the water fountain and the bathroom. (Note that this is not the area where we did our morning meeting activities.) When the last child arrived at the back of the room, I would turn all of the lights off and I would light a candle.

Then the fire marshal came and told me I wasn't allowed to have a candle.

"But I need this candle," I said.

"I'm sorry, but you can't have an open flame in a school," he replied.

"I don't think you understand," I said.

"I don't think *you* understand," he replied. "Just get one of those electric candles."

"It's not the same," I said.

"I don't care," he returned.

So, I got one of those stupid electric candles, but it wasn't the same, and I still pine for the good old days with my real candle. Whatever.

Anyway, I would turn the lights off, and then I would flip the switch on my stupid electric candle. I would quietly tell the children to breathe in ... and breathe out. Breathe in. Breathe out. We would spend a minute just quietly breathing in the dark, watching the (fake) candle flicker out its little light. If someone talked, I would just start my internal timer over (the children learn quickly that this isn't the time to talk). After a minute of sitting in silence, breathing, I would begin tapping children on the shoulder and sending them over to the carpet area. They would proceed in silence and wait in silence until everyone was on the carpet. Then, I would come to my place on the carpet and begin our morning meeting. I have to tell you, there is something almost magical about being in a room with twenty-five insane five-year-olds just breathing and being calm.

---

* Like "Love Train" by the O'Jays or "Walking on Sunshine" by Katrina and the Waves

This little ritual serves a few different purposes. First, and obviously, it divides our classroom community temporally from what comes before. Even if you start out having the worst day, this minute puts a period on that and starts a new day for you in our classroom community. It signals the beginning of being in an environment with your fellow buccaneers, where you know you will be loved and cared for and supported, no matter what.

Second, the quiet and the breathing give the children an opportunity to calm themselves and reset. Just as importantly, the quiet and breathing give *you* a chance to reset. We often think about our students having tough mornings, but, real talk, sometimes we are the ones who have that tough morning. It's reassuring to us to know that, even when we can't quite get the day started right, our community is waiting with calm breath to lift us up in our own difficult moments.

Finally, this little ritual is a reminder of what our class *can* do. The first time I ever went downhill skiing, I found it terrifying. You strap these two planks of waxed wood to your feet and begin sliding down a mountain. The first time you do it, they tell you to put your skis in a pizza shape to slow yourself down or stop. Here's the thing, though—that only really works on the bunny slope. On anything steeper, gravity is going to overcome that, and you begin moving faster and faster and faster. You don't have a grasp on how to turn, so as you pick up speed, your cortisol level just goes up and up and up. Eventually, you panic and intentionally fall down. The second weekend I went skiing, instead of strapping on my skis right away, I watched what good skiers were doing. None of them were using the pizza. When they wanted to stop, they did what is known as a hockey stop, where you turn your skis perpendicular to the slope and dig your upper edges into the snow. Doing this causes you to come to a complete stop (and sprays snow on anyone standing downhill of you). I decided that I was going to master that skill before doing anything else. It took a morning of hard work and falling down, but I did it. From then on, I knew that, no matter how fast I started going, I could stop myself whenever I wanted.

Teaching in a roomful of crazy kids is a lot like skiing for many of us. Things get faster and wilder and crazier, and the actions that we sometimes think should slow this down don't work as well as our professors told us they would. Our cortisol levels go up and up and up, and we begin to panic. Sometimes, we "intentionally fall down" by yelling at our students or losing our tempers. It stops us, but it also incurs damage, not to our bodies but to our relationships. Being able to get every child completely silent is the hockey stop of teaching. It reminds us that we can reset whenever we want, and it keeps us from panicking when things get a little too loud or crazy.

Starting the day with the candle and the breathing are like doing a hockey stop every day after you first strap on your skis. It reminds you that you are in control. You can allow the children to practice self-regulation throughout the day, knowing that they will fail but also comfortable in the knowledge that you can regain control for yourself and your class whenever you wish.

HOW WE REMEMBER THINGS

All of this, of course, brings us to the next logical thing to talk about: colonoscopies. A colonoscopy, if you are unfamiliar, is a procedure wherein a qualified medical doctor takes a long tube with a light and a camera on the end of it and shoves it up your butt in search of cancer. We are currently living in what I like to think of as the golden age of colonoscopies. Nowadays, if you are having this procedure done,* you mix a whole bottle of Miralax in with your favorite beverage as a breakfast treat, spend a day pondering how your bathroom would look with more attractive wallpaper, and then go into the doctor's office for the procedure. They put you into what they call twilight sleep,** do the procedure, and then notify you of the results.

There was a time not so long ago when colonoscopies were performed without any anesthesia whatsoever. I am told by those who experienced colonoscopies during that period that the procedure was incredibly painful and deeply uncomfortable. Psychologists and behavioral economists are never ones to pass up an opportunity to learn from others' pain and discomfort, so they decided this was the perfect chance to learn about how we construct memories.

What do I mean by "construct memories"? Take a second and think about the best vacation you ever went on. Think about where you went and who you went with. What did you do? What did you eat? What did you see? Have you got it in your head? Okay, now, on a scale from one to ten, how good was that vacation? I hope that you are thinking something between eight and ten. (If you aren't, please send me an email, and we can talk about where you should go on vacation.) Next, I want you to start thinking about some of the individual moments from that vacation. Think about going through the airport or the long car ride or when you stubbed your toe against the

* And if you are forty-five or over, you should absolutely be having it done.

** If you are not of an age to have had a colonoscopy, twilight sleep is what they put you in for wisdom teeth extraction as well. It's not full anesthesia, but you don't experience or remember anything while you are under.

doorstop in your hotel room. Was every moment of that vacation an eight or a nine or a ten? Probably not, unless your TSA pat down was qualitatively better than all mine have been. Even though every moment wasn't an eight or a nine or a ten, you think about the whole vacation as being really good.

That's what I mean by constructing memories. We live out our lives in tiny, instantaneous slices of time, but when we think back on things, we group these slices together to form cohesive wholes. These researchers wanted to understand how we assign value to those whole memories, and these colonoscopies performed without anesthesia provided the perfect opportunity.

The researchers, Donald Redelmeier and Nobel Prize winner Daniel Kahneman (1996), gave these colonoscopy patients a small device that allowed them to indicate their level of pain and discomfort at a particular moment on a scale from one to ten. Each minute, the device would prompt them to input a number. A month after the procedure, the researchers followed up and asked patients to remember and rate their level of pain and discomfort during the procedure as a whole. Prior to the experiment, the researchers didn't know what was going to happen. Would it be better for the doctors to go slow, causing low levels of discomfort and pain over a long period, or would it be better to just rip the proverbial Band-Aid off and get after it, even if doing so resulted in higher levels of pain and discomfort over a shorter time span?

It turns out that, out of all the numbers that each participant dialed in over the course of the procedure, only a few of them mattered. If you take the highest number and average it with the average of the last three minutes of the procedure, you end up getting a strong predictor of participants' recollection of the overall procedure. Let's do a little light math to illustrate. If there was a particularly bad moment in the middle (pain at a 10), but the end was not too bad (pain at a 2), the participant would likely rate their memory of that procedure as a 6 (10 + 2 = 12, 12 ÷ 2 = 6). On the other hand, if the doctor snagged the tube right before pulling it out (10), causing extreme pain in the last few minutes of the procedure (10), the patient would remember the procedure as being a 10 on the pain and discomfort scale, even if it hadn't been that bad before this occurred.

What are the big takeaways here? The first one is that the end of a thing has an outsize effect on how we remember that thing. One of the counterintuitive findings of the study I just mentioned is that now, if a doctor is performing a procedure such as a colonoscopy, and they cause the patient a lot of pain right before the end, best practice indicates that they should extend the procedure unnecessarily. They should leave the tube in, causing low levels of pain and discomfort for a few more minutes before removing it. I find that fascinating. When doctors follow this procedure, patients rate the procedure as being better than when they just get it over with a few minutes earlier.

Alright, let's step back to our vacation planning. Let's say that I'm going to Walt Disney World in Florida with my wife, and we decide to leave our son at home with his grandparents. There are four parks at Walt Disney World: Magic Kingdom, Epcot, Hollywood Studios, and Animal Kingdom. Pop quiz: Which park is the best one to go to without children? The objectively correct answer is Epcot.* On which day should I schedule our visit to Epcot? If you have been paying attention, then you know that I should schedule it for the last day. Doing so will cause me to remember my entire vacation more fondly. The lesson here, of course, is that as you plan your own vacations, if you have a choice between doing something that could be fun on the first day or the last day, you should choose the last day.

Now, what does all this have to do with our classrooms? I want us to go back to Fun Friday. You will recall that, in my first year teaching, I did Fun Friday with only the "good kids" attending. The members of the Matthew Club, even before its formation, were generally stuck in my classroom, practicing handwriting at the end of the day on Friday. Unbeknownst to me, this one decision probably caused them to remember every week as being horrible, even when we had good days earlier in the week. By contrast, later in my teaching career, I let everyone come to Fun Friday, no matter what. We would have popsicles on the veranda behind my classroom in the summer and hot chocolate and stories on the carpet during the winter. No matter what the season, we would always end our Fun Friday with a dance party.

The effects of this shift were palpable. Over time, week after week, the children remembered every week as being better than it actually was. Their blending of the individual moments was putting greater weight on the Fun Fridays and less on the Difficult Moment on Tuesday when the Kids Broke Three Mason Jars and Mr. Holland Lost It a Bit. The point here, of course, is to think long and hard about how you end things, be they days or weeks or years. The end of each day should be the best part of the day. The end of each week should be the best part of the week. The end of the school year should be the best part of the year. My principal used to put a lot of pressure on us (I suspect because administrators at our district's central office

---

* If you said anything else, your answer is bad, and you should feel bad! I'm kidding.**

** But seriously.

put pressure on her) to spend every moment of the year teaching, with a particular emphasis on the last few days of the school year. This idea, however, creates a short-term gain, long-term loss situation. Pressure put on teachers dominoed down to children, leading everyone to be unhappy the last few days of the year. Consequently, when children would think back on the year, these last few days would have a larger-than-expected effect on how they thought about school all through the summer.

A few years ago, I was doing some technical assistance with a school in Vermont. They were struggling mightily with Friday afternoon attendance. Parents were pulling their children out of school at a high rate for vacations, dentist appointments, or even reasons as banal as going to catch a matinee at the end of every week. I recommended that they institute a school-wide Fun Friday policy. Every classroom in the entire elementary school would stop 15 minutes before the final bell and celebrate their week in whatever way they deemed best.

A month after implementing the new policy, I met with the school's leadership team—and they were floored by the results. Their attendance problem on Friday afternoons had vanished. In fact, attendance on Friday afternoons was better than any other time during the week. Why? Children did not want to miss Fun Friday. Parents attempting to schedule other events were brutally rebuffed by children who insisted that they must be in school during that time. I then slyly asked them how Monday attendance was going. One of the members of the leadership team had been concerned that the appointments and vacations would just be shifted to another day, with Monday being the most likely. They told me they were a bit bewildered as to why, but their Monday morning attendance had also improved, as had Monday tardies, and I suspect you know why. Children, as they woke up on Monday mornings and thought back to their previous week, were all remembering school as being a more positive experience than they had been before the Fun Friday policy. Their positive feelings and associations led them to be more motivated to show up on Monday morning.

I think it's also important to highlight what this means for you as a professional. Keeping children focused on the parts of a plant or the *mmmm* sound at the end of a long week is stressful for you. If you are "teaching right up to the bell" as my principal used to say, you are making the last bit of *your* week stressful. How will that affect how *you* remember the week? This part is just as important as how the children remember their weeks. Even now, having been out of the classroom for a few years, my Friday afternoons with my students cause me to see my last couple of years teaching with rose-colored glasses. My memories of the children dancing, laughing, and dripping popsicle juice down their chins are bold and clear, while my memories of the difficult Thursday mornings have faded. Fun Friday is about the children, of course, but it's also about you and taking care of yourself.

SHARED GOALS

I hope that you are beginning to see the power of classroom community. We often think about individual children and their particular learning needs. However, as we have noted, social psychology and organizational psychology teach us that much of our learning and motivation are derived from our status as parts of various groups. When you build cohesion among your class and intentionally develop a shared identity for yourself and the children, you facilitate a host of positive outcomes. In this section, I want to focus specifically on the importance of shared goals. Educational psychologists have spent a significant amount of time and ink discussing individual goals, how we pursue them, and how our thoughts and feelings about those goals affect our learning and behavior. Yet, the goals that we create and pursue alongside others can serve as powerful motivators as well.

Before we get too far into this, I want to make sure we all understand what I mean by shared goals. I do not mean group goals, which are goals that we pursue as part of a group; things like group projects in college, winning a sporting event, or filling the marble jar as a class are all group goals. Each person in the group contributes some part, and the final outcome is a win for the group as a whole.* Shared goals, on the other hand, are just what we are each trying to do individually that we know others in our group are also trying to do. To go back to our discussion of rewards and punishments, the outcomes of pursuing these goals will often flow naturally from their accomplishment rather than featuring treats or trinkets.

In chapter 9, we will discuss how to arrange these goals in your classroom environment. However, I wanted to start you thinking about it now, because shared goals also build cohesion among you and your class. Moreover, when these goals are related to things such as self-regulation, having them in common and out in the open will improve the likelihood that children exhibit the behaviors you want to see. Being part of a group that is trying or working on something supports the behaviors of each individual child in that group (Shteynberg and Galinsky, 2011).

---

* Group goals can be powerful as well, but they are also often more difficult to coordinate and leverage as a teacher.

This, in turn, will form a key part of your classroom's culture. Over time, the culture will become larger than any one person in the group, including you. I remember one year I had a child move to my school and classroom in the middle of the year. I do not know what was going on before he arrived, but it was clear from the way he behaved in the classroom that his prior situation was very different. The first morning he was there, we lit the candle and started breathing. He loudly proclaimed, "This is stupid!" If it were possible for silence to be any more silent, that's what happened. Without a word, every other child in that room opened their eyes and looked over at him like he had peed on the floor. I didn't tell them to. They were just so shocked that someone would violate our group culture like that. It only took a few weeks for him to find his way and to learn how we thought and acted and treated one another. If I had been trying to intentionally teach all those behaviors, it would have taken a lot longer. The power of a real classroom community, with its shared goals and culture, is real. Build one with care and intentionality, and you will set yourself and the children up for success for the remainder of your time together.

BEYOND THE CLASSROOM WALLS

In the early '90s, medical malpractice lawsuits were becoming an increasing burden for doctors, hospitals, and insurance companies. However, these groups were all unsure what was causing the suits in the first place. There was no strong correlation between negative medical outcomes and the likelihood of a lawsuit. If you think about it for a second, that's a crazy thing to say. It feels like negative medical outcomes should be the only predictor of whether or not someone sues their doctor. That simply was not what was happening. Plenty of patients were experiencing negative medical outcomes and electing not to sue. A researcher named Howard Beckman and his colleagues, Kathryn Markakis and Anthony Suchman (1994), began examining depositions from medical malpractice lawsuits at a large hospital.

In examining the depositions, they found that the missing piece was the patients' relationship with the doctor. When doctors were perceived to be dismissive or uncaring and made a mistake, patients sued them. When doctors were perceived to be attentive and caring but made a mistake, patients elected not to sue them. Ten years later, researcher Nalinl Ambady and her colleagues (2002) confirmed Beckman's group's finding by examining tiny snippets of conversations between surgeons and patients. Listening to only twenty seconds of conversation between the surgeon and the patient, Ambady's group found that surgeons with a more dominant tone of voice were more likely to be sued, while those with a more concerned tone were less likely to be served with a malpractice suit.

I originally learned about this line of research from Malcolm Gladwell's *Blink: The Power of Thinking Without Thinking* (2005), which I read while teaching kindergarten. As soon as I read about the malpractice research, I understood much about what had been occurring in my interactions with parents during my teaching career.

During my first two years teaching, I adhered to my principal's guidelines for parent interactions, which I strongly suspect were driven by a desire to avoid ending up on the front page of the newspaper. I kept them as professional as possible. My communications were all couched in the language of schools. I avoided seeing or talking to parents and families outside of school hours. When I spoke to them during school hours, I kept things as objective and dry as possible.*

Looking back, it would be hard to be more wrong in how I communicated with parents about their children, and the results spoke for themselves. I had a grandmother drag herself out of a hospital bed at one point to come to the school and accuse me of "hating" her granddaughter. I had another parent, a teacher herself, tell me that she didn't think I belonged in the profession. A third parent came and spent fifteen minutes screaming at me for doing nothing in my class all day. (Said parent asked his child each day what she did at school, to which the child replied, "Nothing." He took the six-year-old at her word.) By the time I left the classroom, however, I had completely turned things around, being elected the PTA Teacher of the Year for the school.

What changed? I started doing the opposite of what my principal had originally encouraged me to do. Rather than keeping families at arm's length, I brought them as close as possible. I created an open-door policy in my classroom, inviting them to spend time with us even if they were not volunteering or leading a learning group. I communicated relentlessly with families about how much I loved and appreciated their children, starting the first week of school. My assistant and I planned monthly Mr. Holland's Class Outings to parks, plays, splash pads, and bowling alleys.

The classic mistake I had made as a new teacher was viewing parent communication as part of my job. Because it was part of my job as a professional, I kept everything professional. However, for parents, schooling and childcare are not professional environments. Rather, they are *intensely* personal. Trying to be professional just

---

* Moreover, as we have previously covered in the Matthew Club story, I was a bit of a snitch.

made me come off as dominant and callous. Sending more criticisms (snitching) than appreciations made it seem as though I saw their children as problems to be solved.

As I began to understand the power of my own classroom community, I also came to understand the importance of including families in it. Families, in my view, shifted from being the cause of problems in the classroom or barriers to solving them to critically important partners. As experts on their children, they provided me with insights that would have taken me months to glean on my own.

I became a trusted resource for them because they understood that I cared about their children, just like they did. They understood this not because of what I told them but because of what I showed them. On the occasion that I did need their support in helping a child through some challenging behavior, they were happy to give it because they saw the request as arising from a desire to do what was best for their child rather than what was best for me. When children would predictably respond to "What did you do today?" with "Nothing," they would come and ask me about it instead of assuming that their child was correct. Many of them had spent time in my classroom, so they knew their child's blow-off answer to be false, but even those whose work schedules did not allow this had enough respect for me to give me the benefit of the doubt.*

In the end, I found that the research on medical malpractice was just as relevant to me as to doctors. Parent satisfaction and engagement were predicted not by my quality as a teacher but rather by parents feeling that I cared for and about their children. Once they understood that, they often forgave small failings and mistakes. They assumed positive intent and leaned into our relationship with one another.

From a principal's perspective, I can understand why my administrator wanted us to keep families at a distance, but in the end, research suggests that this strategy will only increase the likelihood of being on the front page of the newspaper. Having personal (but not inappropriate) relationships with families is the only way to have an effective classroom community.**

Even if we seek to define these communities as temporally existing within the school hours, we must not underestimate the importance of families as active participants in

---

* An important point here for working with children and adults: Respect is not assigned by a position. It is earned through mutual trust and care.

** Note that, in order for this to work, you have to have positive relationships with everyone; otherwise, it just looks like you are showing favoritism. Be mindful of families whose work schedules or transportation situations put them at risk of not having a strong relationship with you and find ways around those barriers, even if it's just a brief text or picture from the classroom every few days.

the group. Their support for and knowledge of their children ensure that, like us, they will be there (mentally, if not physically) in the good times and the bad, the hard times and the good. We will rely on them to lift us up in hard times just as we will lift them up when the going gets tough. In weaving these connections between families, children, and ourselves, we stand the best chance of fulfilling children's need for relatedness with one another in our classroom communities.

* * *

Children have a fundamental need for relatedness. While we as teachers often understandably focus on fulfilling that need ourselves, we have tremendous power to set up a classroom community that facilitates its fulfillment between children as well. In this chapter, we have explored some of the big ideas for shifting children's perspectives on their roles and responsibilities toward one another. In the next chapter, we will move away from fulfilling children's need for relatedness and begin discussing how we can create classrooms that fulfill their need for autonomy. Should we fail to do so, they will find their own ways to fulfill their need for autonomy, to the detriment of our own goals.

CHAPTER 6: SUPPORTING AUTONOMY

Food on the Floor

Get busy living, or get busy dying.

—ANDY DUFRESNE,
THE SHAWSHANK REDEMPTION

Seemingly every Sunday afternoon, *The Shawshank Redemption* plays on TNT. If you are a younger reader, nothing I said after the comma in the previous sentence may make any sense to you. Based on a Stephen King short story, *The Shawshank Redemption* is a movie that came out in 1994 and promptly flopped.* However, the critics loved it, and it was nominated for the Best Picture Oscar. Over time, it grew into a cult classic at least in part because, as you may have heard, it played every Sunday afternoon on TNT. TNT stands for Turner Network Television. It was a cable TV station owned by a billboard-magnate-turned-de facto Sultan of Atlanta Ted Turner. If you don't know what cable TV was, then I don't know what to tell you. Go ask your grandparents, I suppose.

Anyway, *The Shawshank Redemption* plays every Sunday afternoon on TNT, which is now a streaming service. One specific Sunday afternoon, I had gone over to my parents' house for lunch, and my dad and I were watching *The Shawshank Redemption* on TNT. This was probably my fifth year or so in the classroom, and I was multitasking. While the movie was on in the background, I was reviewing some classroom observation data that had been taken in my room. The data showed that I was spending upwards of an hour and a half each day on transitions—cleaning up, lining up, waiting for children outside the bathroom. Like most teachers who get that kind of news, I was desperately trying to figure out how to get that number down.

Now, if you haven't seen the movie, I don't want to spoil it for you because it's a banger. Please go watch it. However, if you're not in a position to do that, I understand. Here's a short, mostly spoiler-free synopsis.

In 1947, banker Andy Dufresne (played by Tim Robbins) is convicted of murdering his wife. He is sent to Shawshank prison in Maine. While there, he becomes friends with Ellis "Red" Redding (played by Morgan Freeman), who has already been in prison for a while due to a crime he committed when he was younger. Over the next twenty years, the men form a close bond. After all that time, though, Red is verging into old age. Having spent his entire adult life in prison, he finally gets out on parole. When he leaves prison, he has a lot of trouble adjusting to life on the outside. Who he is as a person is who he was in prison. The things he is good at are the things he was good at in prison. It's difficult for him to re-orient himself to a life that is much more open and fast-paced than what he is used to.

So, I'm sitting on my parents' sofa, watching the movie with one eye and looking at my classroom data with the other, when I come to a part near the end of the movie

* Competing against *Pulp Fiction* and *Forrest Gump* will do that to a film.

where Red is bagging groceries. He raises his hand and says something like, "Hey boss, can I use the bathroom?" His boss comes over and says, "You don't have to ask permission. Just go." Red looks mystified because his whole adult life he's had to ask for permission to go to the bathroom. As I'm watching this, it hits me like a ton of bricks falling on my head that the only two places in America where you have to ask for permission to go to the bathroom are schools and prisons.

It was one of those crystallizing moments where you just sit back, eyes wide, and have to reflect. I remember clearly thinking that I tell my students all the time that they are strong, capable, independent learners, but I'm not even trusting them to take care of their most basic human needs. I decided in that moment that things needed to change. I was going to kill two birds with one stone: I was going to stop taking children to the bathroom down the hall and stop making them raise their hands when they needed to use the bathroom.

The next morning, as we sat down for morning meeting, I said, "Hey, everyone, I've got some exciting news. From now on, whenever you need to go to the bathroom, you can just go." Now, some of you are experienced teachers, and you anticipate the result that young Adam did not. No sooner had those words left my mouth than twenty-five kindergarteners immediately sprinted for the back of the room. We ended up in a bit of a Three Stooges situation (again, ask your grandparents), with three kindergarteners wedged into the door and the other twenty-two piled up behind them trying to shove them in. I recovered as quickly as I could and called everyone back to the carpet. When everyone had returned and we had done a little deep breathing to reset ourselves, I asked them, "What just happened?"

One of the children said, "We were all trying to get into the bathroom at the same time, Mr. Holland."

I said, "Yeah, what's the problem with that?"

That same child replied, "Well, if we're all back there, pushing and shoving, you can't keep us safe if you're up here by yourself."

I said, "That's a great point. Any other issues?"

Another child piped up and said, "If you're up here by yourself, you can't teach us what we need to learn."

"Brilliant," I said. "Now what are we going to do about it?"

"Well," said the first kid, "there's only one potty in the bathroom, so only one person can go to the bathroom at a time."

"Okay, that sounds good," I responded. At this point, I was finally thinking through things like I should have done from the beginning, so I followed up with this: "What if more than one person needs to go at the same time?"

"The sink is outside the bathroom," a third child added, "so we can stand up if we need to go, and when the kid who is in the bathroom comes out to wash their hands, we can go next."

"Great!" I said. "Let's see how things go."

For the remainder of my teaching career, I didn't have any issues with the bathroom.* I also cut way down on my transition time, as I didn't have to take the children to the bathroom out in the hall anymore.

KNOW THYSELF

In the prior two chapters, we focused on fulfilling children's need for relatedness, first with ourselves and then with other children. In this chapter, we will turn our attention to fulfilling children's need for autonomy. By fulfilling children's need for autonomy, we allow them to take control of their own lives in ways that work for us in our classrooms. When we fail to do so, children will seize control of what is happening around us in ways that may not be okay with us, creating friction and conflict that can undermine everything we have worked for in building our relationships with them. (You will remember that the technical term for this is *maladaptive behavioral patterns*.)

To come back to our *Shawshank Redemption* situation, it illustrates some important points that we will want to consider as we think about how to fulfill children's need for autonomy in the classroom. I often think of autonomy and control as existing along a spectrum. My first year teaching, for example, when I lined my students up, I would have them stand on a specific square with one hand on their hips and one finger on their lips. They were not allowed to talk and had to keep their eyes forward at all times. I was, in this scenario, exerting almost full control. Children were not able to

* Beyond the occasional child singing *High School Musical* songs too loudly while using the facilities, but that's a self-correcting lesson because everyone laughs when you come out.

make any choices about anything when they were lining up or moving from place to place. At the other end of the spectrum, I walked into a classroom and told a bunch of five-year-olds that they could use the bathroom whenever they wanted, with no caveats or boundaries.

Danger lies at both ends of the spectrum. My first year, I dealt with almost constant misbehavior in the line. There are two reasons for this. First, when we set the boundaries of what is acceptable so tightly, *almost anything* counts as misbehavior. If simply turning your head to the side is unacceptable, five-year-olds are going to be constantly crossing your boundaries. Second, as we have learned from our study of self-determination theory, when children's needs are not fulfilled by the environment, they will develop maladaptive behavioral patterns. That is, they will find ways to have autonomy that are not okay with you.

On the flip side, young children *need* boundaries. Part of helping children feel safe in your space is letting them know that you are thoughtful about doing your two jobs. In ensuring they have safe bodies and happy hearts and teaching them what they need to learn, you will need to put fences around what is allowed. Those fences are evidence of your care and support. Children will naturally push against them, as part of growing up is finding your own space to exert autonomy, but finding nothing against which to push is something that can give a three-, four-, or five-year-old a lot of anxiety.

I wish I could end this chapter by listing exactly how you should do everything in your classroom to maintain an optimum balance of giving the children autonomy and setting clear, reasonable boundaries. Unfortunately, I can't do that. Every teacher is different, and what drives one of us crazy is totally fine with another. The initial reaction of many parents and teachers upon first entering my room was that it was chaotic and disorganized. I hope, this far into the book, you will understand that many of the decisions I was making that led to this level of energy were intentional. I was comfortable allowing noise and active bodies in many situations because I felt that the benefits outweighed the costs. In your own spaces, you should not blindly adopt what I was doing, which was comfortable for me. Rather, put boundaries where *you* are comfortable. Trying to be chill about things that you are not actually chill about because others are is a recipe for stress and frustration. As Socrates, from *Bill and Ted's Excellent Adventure*, once said, "Know thyself."

For example, I was not comfortable letting the children sit wherever they wanted on the carpet. When I first started teaching, I would let them sit wherever. Time and time again, however, I found that they made the worst possible choices. If there was a child who needed close supervision and some assistance focusing on me, they would sit at the back of the group. If a child had a particular frenemy with whom they were likely to be disruptive and fight, they would sit together eleven times out of ten, guaranteed. To combat this issue, I picked where the children sat on the carpet every day.*

Once you know where your boundaries are, it is important then to think about how, within those boundaries, you give children opportunities for autonomy. What are the choices children are allowed to make while still adhering to your guidelines? Let's think about my carpet example for a second. I often see teachers give children assigned seats on the carpet. Then, they pair this with telling children their seating position (criss-cross applesauce), to catch a bubble (code for shut your mouth), put your hands in your lap, and look at me. Where is the autonomy? Something has to (and will) give.

Instead of relying on children to somehow self-regulate every single part of their body while also paying attention to the content I was trying to deliver, I set some boundaries that allowed them much more autonomy than this. Children had to be upright on their spot, but they could sit how they wanted. We even talked about different styles of seating so they would have some choices to think about when they needed a new position: straight and narrow, side saddle, cannonball, and so on. Children could do what they wanted with their arms and hands as long as they were not touching others.

I also had two baskets of fidgets near the carpet. If you are unfamiliar, fidgets are small toys that children can manipulate with their fingers. Mine were toys such as Tangles, Rubik's Cubes, and Monkey Rings. The type that I often see, which I would advise avoiding, is stress balls. Anything that can roll is absolutely going to roll and cause a distraction. My boundary for fidget toys was that you could get or trade a fidget toy during transitions but not during whole-group time. This allowed children who maybe wanted to try something new or forgot to grab a fidget first thing to know that a time was coming soon when they could solve their problem without disrupting instruction. Allowing children to quietly play with a toy is helpful for lots of reasons, particularly for children who struggle with executive functions. And fidgets allow all children another opportunity for autonomy during whole-group time.

To sum up, I choose where children sit on the carpet. I put boundaries in place regarding their body positions to keep them safe and ready to learn. The rest of the

---

* If you remember my candle ritual, I would tap each child on the shoulder at the end of it, and that is the order they would sit in on the carpet circle for the whole day. This order was always intentional, even as it always shifted so that children didn't sit in the same place every time.

decisions about how they are during that time I leave up to them. Again, I want to emphasize that this is what works for me. What works for you may be different, and that's okay. When you find the sweet spot, you will know it, because you will see fewer challenging behaviors and fewer maladaptive behavioral patterns. Keep things too tight, and children will push back. Keep things too loose, and you won't be able to do your two jobs properly.

Now that you understand the paradigm, it's time to start thinking about your practice. Think about your daily schedule, your procedures, and your instruction. It's worth sitting down and spending some time going over these things and thinking about each individually. Where are you allowing autonomy, and where are you putting your boundaries? Are children consistently showing you that they need more autonomy during a given time or procedure? If so, you need to find ways that they can have control over themselves and make decisions that you can live with. Are there places where your boundaries are unclear or where they are not supporting your two jobs? You may need to move those boundaries or provide supports to allow children to better stay within them. We will talk about those supports at length during chapter 9.

SHARED DECISION-MAKING

Having thought deeply about how we support children's autonomy by allowing them to make decisions about themselves, let's turn our attention to how we support our class's autonomy as a whole. We do this by allowing them to shape the classroom community and environment. Think about it this way: How would you feel if your boss dictated everything about your classroom? They told you what furniture to put in it and where to put it. They created a schedule for you and told you what to teach every minute of every day. They said what your classroom name and theme would be, where you were allowed to put your stuff, and even which lights would be turned on or off at certain times of the day. I'm guessing that you and the rest of the practitioners in such a place would quickly begin to chafe, feeling that you needed to find ways to take control of your life during your time at work.

I suspect that children often feel this way, even though they rarely say so out loud. They come into classrooms, and their cubby is assigned. Their seat is assigned. The rules and procedures are already set up. When problems come up, their boss (the teacher) solves them and just tells them what will happen to remedy the situation.

Many of us think back on our childhoods as idyllic times with few of the burdens and responsibilities we now carry. However, the flip side of that coin, to turn a quote of Voltaire and Spider-Man's Uncle Ben on its head, is that with no responsibility comes no power. We long for a time when we had fewer responsibilities, but children long for a time when they have more power. By giving up some of our own control, we can support children's need for autonomy by allowing them to become partners in shaping our classroom community.

There are many ways to do this, and we have already discussed some of them. For example, each year, I would let the children decide the identity of our classroom community.* I would regularly let them vote on options such as center materials, read-aloud books, or science investigations. Perhaps you are already doing some of these things. That's great!

I liked to go even further and regularly co-created solutions to problems with them. Sometimes, we would have a Festivus-style airing of the grievances, where children would talk about things that bothered them in our classroom. This sort of thing takes practice. Three- and four-year-olds just aren't used to thinking critically about what is happening around them. So, particularly near the beginning of the year, I would also talk to them about things that were bothering me.

One year, my students were having a lot of trouble sitting on the carpet. Everything that drives me crazy as a teacher was happening almost constantly every time we sat down together. They were touching each other, pulling hair, taking one another's fidget toys, stepping on fingers, lying down, and moving away from where they were supposed to be. I could feel myself losing hair by the day, so I sat them down one afternoon and told them how I was feeling. I shared all the behaviors I was seeing and told them how it made me feel frustrated and upset because it was making it hard to do my jobs. After describing the problem, I asked them what they thought was causing these issues.** The first answer that came out was that they were uncomfortable.

To be clear, I empathized with them. I taught in public school, so they were sitting on a quarter-inch carpet over a concrete slab. No pad. It was, for someone with a bony keister like me, quite uncomfortable after about three or four minutes. Needless to

* Ponies! Pirates!

** Another thing that makes this work better but requires practice is only allowing children to speak for themselves. They can't tell you why Johnny is doing something. Children can only tell you why they themselves are doing something. In a nonjudgmental atmosphere like this, you often have to help them reframe what they are saying because they love to throw shade and point fingers.

say, I didn't sit on the floor with them. I sat in a big, red camp chair. If you've never seen one, camp chairs consist of a foldable metal frame with canvas stretched across it. Mine was enormous with armrests and cup holders. I didn't have to sit on that uncomfortable floor each day, but I understood what they were getting at.

I helped them tie that feeling to a few of the different behaviors we were seeing and then asked them what they thought we could do about it. I thought they were going to request lice squares* or something like that. Nope. One of my sharpest students immediately piped up, "We want chairs like yours!"

I laughed. It was a pretty audacious request. Then, I explained why they couldn't have them. I told them how large the chair was and explained that if we put that many chairs in a circle, it would take up at least half the room. Usually, they were happy to move along in situations like these, but not this time. This time, they kept at it. They wanted chairs. I suggested that they might pull the chairs from our tables over to the carpet. They said those were uncomfortable. I tried to interest them in the lice squares myself. They weren't having it. In the end, I told them that we would table the discussion. They should keep thinking about possible solutions, and we could come back tomorrow with fresh ideas.

As soon as I got home, I did what any good teacher would do: I tried to figure out how to convince the children that they were wrong.** Problem-solving with kids isn't just about solving problems. It's about helping them see a process. Group problem-solving adds the dynamic of showing them how to carefully consider one another's ideas and also helps them see *why* certain ideas will work and others will not. I ended up deciding that we would make a small-scale model of the classroom, and we would use little pieces of paper to be the chairs. Then, I could show them how much room the chairs would take up, which would leave us with no room for the toys, games, learning materials, and centers that they loved. I could make clear that the costs outweighed the benefits.

I went on the internet to find the dimensions of my camp chair, and as I was browsing to find the correct model, I learned that they make camp chairs for little kids as well. They were just like mine in form and function, only smaller. I remember just staring at the screen. After sitting there for a moment, motionless, the cool light of walmart.com bathing my face, I made the decision. Dadgummit, we were going to get

---

* If you're unfamiliar, lice squares are these little rectangles of bound carpet that teachers like to put out around their circles. Children sit on them—and lice breed in them.

** I'm kidding, of course. Kind of.

those camp chairs. I ended up writing a DonorsChoose grant, spending a little of the stipend our PTA gave us, asking my class parents for some money, and (because this is public education) pitching in some of my own money. I bought twenty-eight little, child-sized camp chairs (three spares in case of damage or breakage).

Listen, dear reader, I need you to understand: This was the best idea I ever got in my entire teaching career, and it came from a five-year-old. I put those camp chairs out in a circle. My students sat down in them, and it was like the Ritalin Fairy came and sprinkled them all with self-regulation dust. They sat still. They were quiet. They looked at me and listened. They ignored one another. It. Was. A. Miracle. I suspect this has something to do with the nature of the chairs; the way the canvas wraps around their little bodies, providing proprioceptive input. Whatever the reason, it was a night-and-day difference. They went from being one of my worst-behaved groups during morning meeting and read-aloud to my best class ever in those situations, and I never would have thought of this myself.

This idea came from one of the children because I had enough faith in them to let them decide how our classroom space was going to be. Over the course of my teaching career, we did a lot of problem solving. For every decent, workable idea, there were five bad ones.* However, I always counted this as time well spent. Our collaborative problem solving helped them understand the nature of problems, showing them that they are not internal and unmovable. Rather, problems are something we can work on together. Over the year, they would learn how to think about the costs and the benefits of particular solutions and make informed decisions. (Since leaving the classroom, I have worked with many adults who never learned to do this.) Finally, and most importantly, I gave them a real voice in how our classroom operated and how their daily lives played out in it, because sometimes autonomy is not just about having a voice in how an individual lives but in enjoying the obligation of building a better community as part of a democratic society.

THE RULES

In addition to our class problem-solving times, one of the other key ways that I gave children agency in deciding how the classroom would be was in allowing them to select the classroom rules. Now, it has become standard practice over the last

* Some of my classes consisted of three-year-olds, so this is to be expected.

twenty years to allow children to choose the rules, so some of you might be saying a big So what? to this. However, I want to be clear that when I say I let the children pick the rules, I mean that I let them pick *all* the rules. Far too many times, I observe classrooms going through this process, and teachers suggest or "like" particular rules that matter to them (such as, be quiet when others are speaking). Then, because children are brown nosers, they pick these rules to be the classroom rules. Teachers get the rules that they wanted while allowing themselves to feel like they gave the children a voice in something, even when they didn't.

What allowed me to give children full autonomy in this regard was my two jobs. Once we had established my jobs (ensuring everyone has safe bodies and happy hearts, teaching everyone what they need to learn) and their job (help me with my two jobs), anything else that I layer on top of this is, to some degree, unnecessary. Every procedure, interaction, problem-solving session, and decision made throughout the year is just a manifestation of one of those two jobs. That rule teachers love to insert, "Be quiet when others are speaking," is just a part of them helping me with job number two. Because everything important is already taken care of, the rules they create can serve as *their* rules. Since I talk about jobs when I am handling issues in the classroom, I also do not need to enforce these rules. I leave that up to them.

To establish the rules each year, I had a fairly simple procedure. First, because I introduced jobs on day one, I did not need to rush into introducing the rules. Rather, I would wait a few weeks, so that children really understood my jobs on a deeper level than they could on week one. In week four or so, I would start our morning meeting on Monday by talking about my two jobs and how it would be nice if they thought about what kinds of rules they might like to set for themselves to help them do their one job. I was clear that these rules would be their responsibility and not mine. Then, I would ask them to tell me a couple of rules that they thought might be important.

Each day, we would consider two or three rules that children suggested. I would take new suggestions and we would agree on phrasing. Then, I would write that rule on a giant sticky note and put it up near our whole-group area. We would discuss the strengths and weaknesses of each rule, thinking about how it would help with jobs, making sure it was reasonable, and deciding how important it was. Often, suggestions later in the week were just different wordings of prior suggestions, so we would decide whether or not a rule was truly novel as well. By the end of the week, we had between ten and fifteen rules to consider. I would make them into a list and send them home over the weekend with a request for parents to read the list and help their children narrow it down to the two that their child thought were most important.

(My instructions to parents also included a clear request not to try to shape their children's opinion of what was important.)

The following Monday during morning meeting, I would give each child two dot stickers and ask them to put the dots on the two rules they felt were the most important for helping them do their job. I never had a hard-and-fast rule for how many votes a rule needed to get to become a classroom rule. I never had more than five rules, and sometimes I only had two or three. I was just looking for a drop off in votes. The fascinating thing about allowing children to pick the rules is that they often don't pick the rules that you would pick. The year that we had only two rules, one of those rules (and the one with far and away the most votes) was Don't put things you find on the ground in your mouth.*

Everyone but me voted for this rule, including my assistant.** One of the children had just learned about germs during the week when we were discussing rules and came to school proselytizing the good word of handwashing and bacterial warfare. The other children immediately got on board and decided that a critical way they were going to keep themselves safe was by preventing the ingestion of germs, hence the rule. Do I think that this rule is important? Of course I do. Would it be one of only two rules I had for a kindergarten class? Absolutely not. Still, it was what they picked, and the proof of the efficacy of this method of letting children pick their own rules was borne out in the actions of my students.

Even into the spring of that year, the children adhered to and were vigilant to enforce this rule. That is something you just don't see when the rules belong to the adults in the room. We would be enjoying a Friday lunch bunch in my classroom in April, and one of the children would drop a cracker onto the floor. They would reach down, pick it up, and move to eat it. If one of the other kids saw this, they would come across the table in slow motion like they were in *The Matrix* and snatch the cracker out of the first kid's hand. Without fail, they would turn their wide-eyed gaze on the would-be cracker-eater and gasp out, "You can't eat that! It's been on the floor!" I never saw a child get mad at this kind of behavior, either. They would just look up at their savior and nod, like they couldn't believe the risk they had nearly taken in a fit of unbridled cracker desire.

This sort of thing, in addition to fulfilling children's need for autonomy, also helped them feel like their job (to help ensure everyone had safe bodies and happy hearts

---

* Yes, I understand that this violates the "Don't phrase rules negatively" rule that is considered best practice, but the children felt that a positive phrasing did not capture what they were going for here.

** Betrayal!

and to help everyone learn what they needed to learn) was not just an extension of my job. This goes back to our classroom community and a sense of shared responsibility. The community is not something that I created and ran. Rather, it was something co-created by all of us and maintained by all of us. I found over the years that this increased buy-in buffered some of the effects a little too much familiarity would have on children's behavior as the year wore on.*

The last thing I will say about having children create the rules is that they often require some assistance in understanding how to sensitively address breaches of the rules. Their default reaction is often anger or frustration (just like many adults!). To overcome this, I spent a lot of time helping them internalize a key value: When we address rule-breaking, we are not trying to help ourselves. Rather, we are trying to help the individual who is breaking the rule. Even if they are swinging a block around, putting others in danger, our intervention in that situation is targeted at moving that child from where they currently are (out of control) to a place where they can be their very best self (in control). Having their perspective be that they are providing assistance helps them understand the correct tone and level of intervention necessary.

Once they understood this perspective of being a helper, then we practiced (over and over) what that looks, sounds, and feels like. We parsed out when they could handle things on their own versus needing assistance from an adult (with the child still taking the lead). We talked about how to open these conversations (speaking for yourself, noticing instead of judging) and how to handle it if things went a little sideways.**

* * *

All of this took time and effort, but I found it to be well worth it. To my point from the opening of the book, this is what it means to be working hard but moving. The time spent crafting and maintaining the children's rules motivated them to engage more fully in the classroom community. It also gave them skills that they could apply to future situations. More on this in chapter 8. Together, these things meant that I was

---

* I know you know what I mean here. I cannot seem to find any scientific basis for this, but every teacher I know has seen that point in January or February when the children have gotten so used to all our procedures and boundaries that they start to try to push against them again, leading to a revival in challenging behavior around this time.

** Sometimes, when someone is doing something that violates the rules, they are not thinking clearly. First, be sure that you are safe. Then, help them calm their body down. Then, you can help them find a better way to do what they are doing or get what they want.

often exhausted at the end of the day, but I could also see the clear progress that the children were making, which tended to make it a good exhaustion, an exhaustion that results from moving forward on a big project rather than the exhaustion of just trying to maintain or stay in the same place. For me, that made all the difference.

CHAPTER 7: SUPPORTING COMPETENCE

Math and Tennis

With such missing data, it is possible that these values are missing completely at random, missing at random (MAR) or missing not at random (MNAR). Older methods of dealing with this issue such as listwise deletion have been shown to lead to spurious conclusions and incorrect inferences when data are MAR or MNAR. However, modern analytic techniques, particularly full information maximum likelihood estimation (FIML), allow researchers to more accurately model data while maintaining optimal type I error rates.

—ADAM HOLLAND, "CHILDREN'S SOCIAL COMPETENCE ACROSS THE TRANSITION TO KINDERGARTEN: A LATENT GROWTH CURVE ANALYSIS"

"Anyone for tennis?"

—ENGLISH IDIOM

My dissertation was a multiple-group latent growth curve analysis of children's social competence across the transition to kindergarten using a large, multistate data set. Did you just throw up in your mouth a little? That's okay. Many do. They just can't handle how excited and engaged they become when they hear about advanced mathematical and statistical techniques. Let's cool it down a little. Matrix algebra. Maximum likelihood. Integrals. No? Still feeling a little queasy?

It's fine. I get it. When I tell people that part of my job is as a statistician and a psychometrician, I get practically the same response from everyone. "Oh, I could never do that. I'm not very good at math."

I could never do that. I'm not very good at math.

There's a lot to unpack in those two little sentences. When I hear people say this, I understand not just how they feel about their own math skills but how they probably feel about ability itself. What they are telling me is that they believe math ability is something that some people have and some people don't. I can do PhD-level structural equation modeling because I have that ability. I was born with it (unlike some Maybelline users you may have heard tell about). They were not.

During that same conversation, I might ask my new friend what they did over the weekend. They might say, "Oh, I actually had my first tennis lesson on Saturday."

"How did it go?" I ask.

"Oh, so badly," they laugh. "I hit more balls over the chain link fence than I did into the court."

"Ah," I say, "so you're going to give it up."

"Of course not," they laugh. "I have another lesson next week. I want to get good enough to play doubles with my partner."

I want to get good enough to play doubles with my partner.

There's a lot to unpack in that one little sentence. What this person is communicating tells me not just about their reason for taking lessons but also their beliefs about tennis ability: Unlike math ability, which is fixed and handed down from on high to some but not others, tennis ability is something one can improve through practice. It's important to understand that these beliefs (that some people are good at math and others are not; that you can improve your tennis ability through hard work and practice) are not mutually exclusive. Because these beliefs are specific to particular domains, someone can believe both simultaneously.

DOMINOES

These two different ways of seeing ability are important because they form the first dominoes in a chain reaction that leads to very different types of motivation and ways to approach learning. Down one domino path, we see children who love learning and challenge themselves to constantly improve. Down the other, we see children who stick to the safe things they know they are good at and may even sabotage their own learning in other domains. In this chapter, we will focus on how to tip the right dominoes to effectively motivate children by fulfilling their need for competence.

FIXED MINDSET

So, we have established two different ways of seeing ability. With one way, children might view their ability as something a person has or doesn't have. I remember, even in second grade, thinking that my friend Alkesh was really smart.* He had an ability to understand everything that the teacher said, no matter how complicated it was. He could read well and add groups of objects together. When he raised his hand to answer a question during story time, I knew that he would produce the correct answer. All this is to say that even young children have these ways of thinking about ability.

Carol Dweck (2006), a researcher at Stanford, called this kind of thinking a *fixed mindset*. People often misinterpret what a fixed mindset is. It does not mean that someone is fixed in their thinking or that they are inflexible. Rather, it refers to how someone thinks about a particular ability. If they believe that ability cannot change and that some people have it while others don't, that is a fixed mindset.

This idea that the ability cannot be changed is key, because it is the first domino. If our ability in a domain (say, math) is fixed, then what happens when we take a math test? What happens is that the math test gives us information. It tells us where our ability level is. If we score well on that test, we have high ability. If we do poorly, we have low ability. The focus is on the outcome or our performance on the task, as that gives us the important information about where our ability level is. When children are primarily focused on doing well on a task such as a test to prove that their fixed ability level is high, researchers call that *performance-approach motivation* (Pintrich, 2000).

---

* Alkesh is now a dentist. Fun dental fact: The modern toothbrush was invented in England. If it had been invented anywhere else, it would be called a teethbrush.

Children with performance-approach motivation often do quite well in school. They study hard and are frequently straight-A students because their goal is to look good in that domain by doing well on outcome-based measures of success such as tests and projects. Unfortunately, there are also children with a fixed view of ability whose goal is similar but conceptually different: to not look bad on these performance outcomes. Researchers call these goals *performance-avoid goals*. Children with these types of goals often take on tasks they are sure they will succeed at rather than pushing themselves to try new or difficult things. Trying a more challenging task might lead to failing and looking bad. If children are averse to doing so, it will be difficult to expand their abilities and skills. Moreover, the desire to not look bad can lead to self-sabotage. Doing so looks something like this: A child is having difficulty with math. A math test is coming up on Friday. No one wants to feel like they are dumb or not good at something, which leads us to look for other reasons for our failure. We seek an external (to us) reason that we did not or will not do well. When the math tests come back with grades attached, the child proudly holds up his D and says to his friends, "I don't care about math at all, so I didn't study for this."

This is red flag number one. Learning is all about pushing ourselves to try new things.*

The reason for the poor grade (according to the child) is not that he is bad at math. Instead, it is that he does not care about math and therefore did not study. This sort of thing often leads to a downward spiral. The poor grades due to not studying lead to a self-belief that the child lacks math ability, which leads to even less studying and even worse grades.

Even in children who have a fixed mindset about an ability and develop mostly performance-approach goals, a more insidious problem is lurking. That problem begins when failure appears. Unfortunately for individuals with a fixed mindset, we all fail eventually. Children might go through their entire schooling career with a fixed mindset about math. They work hard to get good grades on every math test in every class. This motivation drives them to success after success on outcome after outcome. Then, they go to college and take a class on differential equations, and it's hard—really hard. They don't naturally understand everything the professor is saying. The problem sets the teaching assistant assigns for homework are a slog to get through. Even though they study hard, their first test comes back with a disappointing grade: C−.

---

* Except for durian. I wish I had never smelled or tasted it. I regret ever learning anything to do with this demon fruit.

Because this child does not believe that ability level can change, this C– tells them important information. It tells them that they were good at high school math and even basic calculus (all A's in those classes) but that they are not good at college math. They use this information to make a decision to switch out of the math major they had planned to pursue and instead decide to focus on majoring in underwater basketweaving.

Do you see what happened here? Because this person viewed ability as fixed and tests as an indication of ability level, the test gave them information about where their unchangeable ability level was. If you find out you are bad at something you cannot change, what is the only logical way to handle that? It's to give up. After all, there is nothing you can do to change your ability, so why drag yourself through unnecessary torment trying to push through in a domain where you have reached past the point of what you can do well?

This obviously is not ideal in college. We would probably prefer that our children use their college careers to earn a degree in engineering or math over underwater basketweaving.* However, it is even more problematic when it happens in, say, first grade. A child with a fixed mindset who goes through a period of failure in a particular subject or area may decide that they just don't have that particular skill and that's that. Once this happens, it can be difficult to move their thinking back to a growth mindset. Doing so would require some explicit instruction and coaching, but children don't walk around with big signs that say "Fixed Mindset about Math" on them, so knowing that this is something you need to prioritize can be difficult.

GROWTH MINDSET

On the other hand, children with growth mindsets — that is, who believe that abilities or intelligence can improve — approach failure differently. If you believe that something such as math ability can be improved and you do poorly on a test, then you understand that means you need to improve your math ability so you can improve your test scores on future exams. This might mean putting in more effort, trying out some new study techniques, or getting tutoring from a more knowledgeable peer or adult. Children with growth mindsets develop what is called a *mastery orientation* toward the tasks they undertake. Test scores and similar outcomes provide one data point on a lifelong journey toward mastery of a domain rather than an unmovable indication of ability. This is a much more adaptive way to approach temporary

* Apologies if you come from a long line of underwater basketweavers. I'm sure it's a perfectly respectable profession in your neck of the woods.

setbacks or failures. For these children, the focus is on the process rather than the outcome. Successes and failures are both okay, as long as we adapt to them well. Success indicates effective strategies and effort levels. Failure indicates that changes are needed in one or more of these areas.

Because of this, children with fixed mindsets tend to have lower achievement levels than children with growth mindsets over longer time frames. I hope, at this point, you understand why. Children with fixed mindsets about math ability or intelligence in general will develop performance goal orientations; their priority is on outcomes and either looking good on them or at least not looking bad. When failure happens at these outcome-related tasks, they respond by giving up or self-sabotaging. Children with growth mindsets and mastery goal orientations, on the other hand, deal with failure by trying new strategies and working harder. As they overcome temporary challenges and setbacks, this information about their own performance further reinforces their mindset, just as the failures of children who give up reinforce their fixed mindsets.

It's worth taking a moment here to clarify my opinions about ability. I do believe that ability is malleable to a degree. We have more than fifty years of research suggesting that this is the case. For example, one of the projects on which I have had the pleasure to work over the years, the Abecedarian Approach, showed that children who received high-quality care from birth to age five entered school with higher IQs than their peers who did not receive the intervention (Ramey, Sparling, and Ramey, 2012).

I also recognize that there are limits on this malleability. No amount of swimming practice could have turned me into Michael Phelps. The ratio of his torso length to leg length means that he could generate more force in the water than I ever could, even if we both developed our talents at the same rate. These limits, though, rarely come into play for us or our students. I want my children to be competent math students with the opportunity to choose a math-based field of study later in life if that is their wish. I do not need them to win a Fields medal and be recognized as the greatest mathematician in the world. If you see your students' differences in ability, that is fine. We meet children where they are and move them forward. These existing differences do not mean that children are locked into the ability levels they have now. All evidence suggests that abilities and intelligences can grow over the course of a lifetime, given that children receive high-quality instruction.

JUDGMENTS OF COMPETENCE

How do we, then, support children's competence and build within them growth mindsets? Let's start by dipping back into self-determination theory just a bit and combining what we know about that with what we have learned about growth mindset. You will recall that we want children to develop intrinsic motivation rather than external motivations if we can. How do we do that with competence?

We start by having them focus on their internal judgments about their own competence rather than external ones. There are many different ways we can judge our competence on a given task. There is *task-referential competence*, where the task itself gives us all the information we need. When a three-year-old puts a simple puzzle together, if all the pieces fit and it forms the picture on the box, then the child has succeeded. No more feedback is needed.

Other times, children may compare their performance to others or seek the approval of adults. These are external sources of feedback and will tend to yield external motivations. Children will naturally develop these to some degree. For example, if you are working with three children on some basic counting tasks and one child always knows the correct answer, other children in the group will naturally compare themselves to that child. There is nothing wrong with this, and it is largely unpreventable. However, I also see teachers do things that dump gasoline on the nascent fire, and those things we want to avoid. My second-grade teacher, for example, had a large bulletin board on the wall in our classroom that tracked how many timed math fact sheets we had completed. The children in the class who were already good at math flourished under this system, as their comparisons to the other children were always favorable. However, for the children who did not start the year with high math ability, it was discouraging. They were comparing their nascent math abilities with children whose parents had already worked with them on these tasks. They were, in effect, being encouraged to see their competence as something that existed relative to their peers, and the comparison suggested that they had low math ability.

Competence does not need to be defined in relation to others. For many children, school represents the first time that they will consistently compare their own abilities to those of their peers. Prior to this, they will largely compare their ability level to where it existed in the past. This is known as *self-referential competence*. Think, for example, of children who are learning to tie their shoes.* At first, it is difficult. Their growing fine motor skills might not even allow them to move beyond the first part of a bow. As they try to make the loops and manipulate the laces, they fail.

With encouragement from their family members, however, they persevere. They practice the motions over and over. In a week, they are easily tying the half-knot that forms the basis for a bow. A week or two later, they can consistently make two loops and hold them both. Another week later sees them wrapping the loops around one another and pulling one through, forming a rudimentary bow. A final week of hard work, and they can tie a bow that keeps their shoes tight around their ankles. Throughout this process, children are not looking to their peers to understand their level of competence. Rather, they are looking back at their previous abilities. They can see the steady journey of progress as they measure their competence each week against its level during the prior week or month.

One of the key benefits of self-referential competence is that it tends to march in a positive direction. Children don't see themselves as smart or dumb when it comes to tying bows. Instead, they see that they are consistently improving their skills. This is the type of competence we want to support: a competence that grows slowly and steadily toward mastery. How, then, do we as adults focus on leading children toward growth mindsets and mastery goal orientations? Just as we do anything else—intentionally.

SUPPORTING COMPETENCE

As we come near the end of this chapter on competence, I think it is worth spending some time thinking about how we can be intentional about developing growth mindsets and mastery goal orientations in our students. It is tempting to praise children for their ability and intelligence. I see this in the most basic ways when children solve math problems or read their first words in a book, and well-meaning adults say, "Oh, you're so smart!" However, this can also occur with other abilities and in other domains. My son loves to draw, and because he spends hours each day doing so, his pictures include details such as shading and perspective that are rarely

* Once, when I was teaching, one of the children interrupted storytime to ask if I would tie his shoe. Being a benevolent dictator, I agreed to do so. As I began tying, I asked him if he knew why his shoelace was so wet. "Oh yeah," he replied, "I peed on it a minute ago." Shoe tying may not be the most important skill children learn, but it's near the top of my list.

featured in the artwork of other five-year-olds. As I'm writing this, during the last week alone, I heard four adults tell him that he is a talented artist. In the moment, these little nuggets of praise lift children's confidence and feelings of competence. However, in the long run, focusing on children's underlying ability tends to breed a fixed mindset about intelligence or artistic talent.

The second, and perhaps easiest, thing to do is to examine what we are praising and focusing on when we talk to children. Rather than focus on children's abilities, we should focus on the process. This often means two things. First, we want to focus on their grit and drive. We might say something like, "That was really hard, but you kept trying," or "You didn't get that right the first time, but you kept at it until it made sense." We want children to know and understand that failure is okay, and that the way to respond to failure is continued effort.

The second, often overlooked, piece on which we should focus are the strategies children use to move past their failures and difficulties. It is not enough that children keep at it when they fail. If we only promote continued effort, we will end up with children who keep trying the same things over and over, leading to continued failure. Therefore, we want to draw attention to what happens when children fail but try something new and more effective to overcome obstacles. If a child, for example, is having trouble counting a group of objects, we might show them how to pull the objects across the table in front of them as they count to ensure they don't accidentally count the same object twice. When they master the skill, we should draw their attention to the effectiveness of their new strategy and appreciate that they tried something new when they weren't getting the correct answer at first.

These individual areas of focus, of course, should exist within a classroom's system of values. There will be many values you hold high in your classroom, some of which we have already talked about, such as when someone in our classroom community has a difficult moment, we help them. Another one that I would like you to consider is this: It is okay to fail. Failure is not a sign of low intelligence or even poor effort. It is a necessary step on a journey of growth. When we are teaching children to read, we often think about this balance. We want to give children books that have word patterns that they will recognize but also words that they have to struggle a little to figure out. By sounding out these words and applying their knowledge over and over, they get better at reading. It's the stretching and challenge that are important here. Children who read the same three books over and over again because they know all the words never improve. I don't know that we need to go so far as to have failure celebrations, as I've seen in some classrooms, but I do think that it is worth talking matter-of-factly about how failure is an important part of getting better at things.

A key corollary of this is managing the stakes of different activities. When real stakes are on the line, it is almost impossible for us to focus on anything but the outcome. After all, this outcome will decide whether or not we get the job, succeed at our sport, or win the admiration of our peers. Putting a lot of emphasis on doing well on an assessment or a performance can act similarly, convincing children that failure is not an option. This is particularly important when children are competing. Plenty of people advocate for a no-competition model, but I am not one of them. I enjoy a fun sight-word relay or game of Cross the Ocean from time to time. What is important when we are having children compete is to bring the stakes down as low as possible. The focus during competitions should be on the joy of the game rather than the winning or the losing. If children are disappointed about losing, it is a perfect time to remind them of the role of failure in helping us get better.

Optimally, all of these things exist within a context where the focus is on process rather than outcome, so a key way of shifting children toward defining competence as movement forward in that process rather than as an outcome is to let them track their progress. In my own classroom, we used this technique in combination with student-led conferences. Throughout the year, children would do formative assessments with myself or my assistant. They would then record the results in their own journals, which we kept for this purpose. The learning progressions were clearly laid out, so children could see where they were previously and their current level. Other times, we were interested in counts, such as how many letter names, letter sounds, or sight words children knew. We would let them color in a bar that showed their growth. This is very different than having a board in the room where children get a star when they know all the letter names, letter sounds, or sight words. Such boards invite children to compare their performance (and define their competence) in reference to one another. But, when children track their own progress, they are encouraged instead to compare their current level of work to their own work in the past, allowing them to see growth rather than a standard level of achievement.

When we help children define their competence in adaptive ways, putting the emphasis on growth rather than on outcomes, we fulfill their need in ways that will prove adaptive in the long term. Eventually, everyone fails at something. It turns out that how we react to that failure is pretty important, as that response can either push us forward or lead us to stagnate. Whether we are talking about behavior, academics, or something else entirely, we should be mindful to put children in the best position possible to make failure a springboard rather than a roadblock. In doing so, we fulfill their need for competence and lead them toward positive functioning, positive development, and a positive sense of well-being, laying the foundation for the teaching we will be doing in the next chapter.

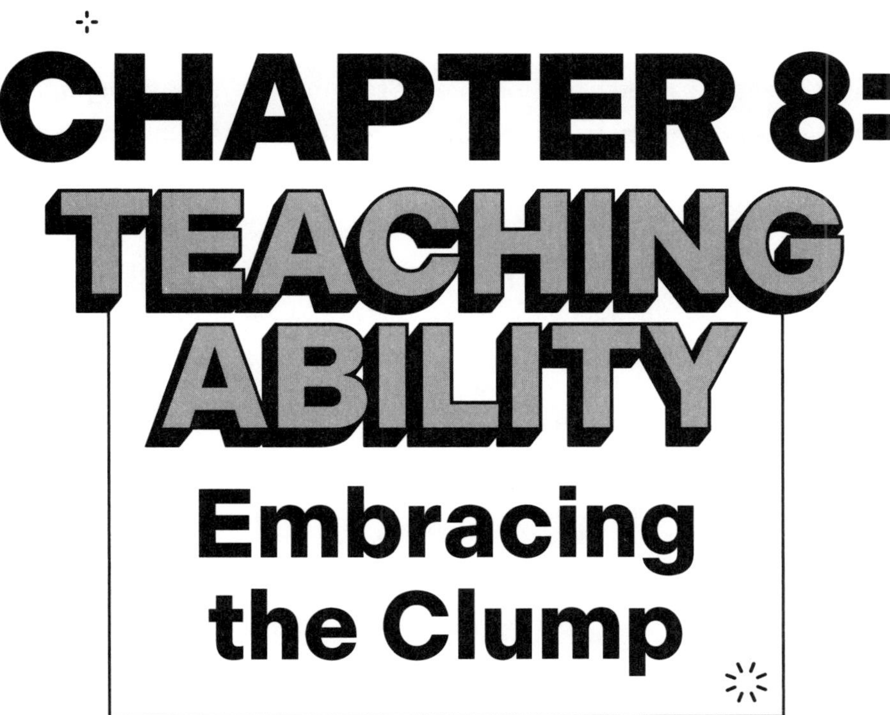

CHAPTER 8: TEACHING ABILITY

Embracing the Clump

**Training is everything.
The peach was once a bitter almond;
cauliflower is nothing but cabbage
with a college education.**

—MARK TWAIN,
AMERICAN AUTHOR AND HUMORIST

In his 2008 book, *Outliers: The Story of Success*, Malcolm Gladwell popularizes the idea that what separates novices from experts is down to a single variable: practice. Specifically, Gladwell proposes that what unites experts is that they have put 10,000 hours of practice into their area of expertise, be that music, sports, programming, or science. In the intervening years, the idea has taken hold in the public consciousness. Like many simple ideas, it has spread far more quickly than the ideas on which this proposition was originally based. Now, I often meet people who know the "10,000 hour rule" but do not even know that it was popularized by Gladwell or that it is originally based on research spanning from the 1970s to the present on subjects as varied as music and chess.

Unfortunately, there is little to no evidence that such a rule actually exists. Some researchers believe that 10,000 hours indicates the minimum amount of practice required to reach a base level of mastery; others emphasize that the true amount of time varies according to other factors, such as the aptitude of the individual or the particular field in which they are seeking mastery. Understanding expertise will require us to dig a little deeper, so let's begin with Anders Ericsson and his colleagues, the researchers on whose work Gladwell based some of his insights. In 1993, Anders Ericsson, Ralf Krampe, and Clemens Tesch-Römer published an article entitled "The Role of Deliberate Practice in the Acquisition of Expert Performance." The article involves an investigation of violin and piano players. Ericsson and his colleagues attempted to understand what separates really, really good players from true masters. The most important finding was a simple one. Over the many years of their careers, the best musicians accumulated more hours of practice.

All this says that practice really does move us closer to perfection. Before we go too far, however, we must define what *practice* or, as it is termed in the literature, *deliberate practice*, means. In a 2008 article on the topic, Ericsson defines it as such: "Significant improvements in performance were realized when individuals were 1) given a task with a well-defined goal, 2) motivated to improve, 3) provided with feedback, and 4) provided with ample opportunities for repetition and gradual refinements of their performance." What I hope you notice here is that deliberate practice is not simply doing a task a lot. Rather, multiple key pieces must be present for an activity to qualify.

In fact, you might notice that the four pieces of deliberate practice are remarkably close to how we teach children. If I want children to be able to add two sets of objects together, that forms my goal. I help them understand the importance of knowing this skill. As they work on it, I ask questions to understand what they are thinking, providing feedback to them accordingly to correct misconceptions or help them employ new strategies.* Finally, we repeat this process over and over, so they gradually improve.

Deliberate practice is not just important for becoming an expert. It is important for developing basic competence. If we want children to learn reading, writing, 'rithmetic, science, technology, engineering, math, social studies, or really any subject, this is how we should go about it. It is not enough that children spend hours engaging with numbers or letters or books. If we want them to develop math and literacy skills, we must intentionally teach them the knowledge they need and then how to use that knowledge to develop skills in these areas.

Sometimes, I do work with schools and districts on both pedagogy (how we teach) and challenging behavior. I generally give them a choice of what they want to learn first. Nine times out of ten, they choose challenging behavior, which often leads me to ask why they chose that order. Inevitably, what district and center leaders tell me is that the teachers are struggling so much with challenging behavior that they need to solve that issue before we can move on to teaching. That is, they see behavior as a prerequisite for teaching. This is, unfortunately, the wrong way to view challenging behavior.

JUST LIKE ANY OTHER SUBJECT

The correct way to understand challenging behavior is to see it as any other subject. This chapter is about changing children's abilities. To change children's abilities requires intentional teaching and deliberate practice. Just as we teach literacy, math, science, and social studies, we must start deliberately teaching behavior. We have to impart knowledge, tie that knowledge into children's existing knowledge, help children understand when and where to apply that knowledge, give them opportunities to practice, and provide helpful feedback throughout. In doing so, we guide them toward mastery.

We do this for other subjects, but we often fail to do this for behavior. To illustrate, I want you to imagine that you walk into a one-room schoolhouse in 1945.

---

* I should note that the quality of the feedback matters. It is not enough to say *right* or *wrong*. Rather, we must help children understand what their misconception is, correct it, and then show them how to apply the new way of thinking. This is not a book about pedagogy, per se, but I will give you this tip for free. Being in a hurry while teaching a group of students and not taking the time to do this is the single most common mistake I see teachers make.

The schoolmarm is just beginning a math lesson on simple addition. She writes a problem on the chalkboard at the front of the room, and the children copy the problem onto their slates. The children then diligently try to solve the problem while the teacher circulates around the room. Children who get the problem correct receive gold stars and pats on the head. Children who get the problem wrong receive a wrap on the knuckles from the teacher's ruler. If a child has gotten a few problems in a row wrong, they may be sent via a pointed finger to go sit on a stool facing the corner and wear a conical hat with the word *Dunce* written on it. Then, the process is repeated. During this entire time, no one in the classroom utters a word. So, is this a good way to teach math? If not, what is wrong with it?

I run through this scenario and ask this question of educators all the time. I have never had anyone seriously answer that they feel like this is an effective pedagogical technique for math instruction. The reasons that teachers and administrators give me for why this is ineffective all tend to converge on one answer. The children are learning whether they are right or wrong, but the teacher is not giving them any information on why they are right or wrong or telling them what to do instead. By the end of the thought exercise, I often have a group of educators who feel a sense of smug superiority—until I remind them that this is how I watch most teachers teach behavior.

Frequently, when children do the wrong thing, all the feedback they get is their name pronounced with a particular verbal inflection that lets them know they have stepped out of line. They are asked to go flip a card, move a clip, or go to another center. Sometimes, they'll ask what they did wrong. As often as not, the answer will be, "I think you know." For me, sitting at the back of these classrooms, this all feels so eerily similar to the schoolmarm's approach. Children get feedback, but it is not the sort that helps.

I imagine that it is like trying to learn a complicated sports motion, such as hitting a golf ball with a driver. You watch other people who have practiced for years launching golf balls off the tee up and down the range. It looks easy, natural. When you try, however, the ball sputters off the mat in front of you or immediately shanks to the left. With each swing, your instructor stands behind you, saying your name with that same sharp, exasperated tone. When you turn around to ask what you did wrong, they just say, "I think you know." It has to be so frustrating. You know you're doing it wrong, but there is a considerable gap between knowing you are wrong and being able to do it right.

We have to do better. When we think about subjects such as literacy or math, we understand that children will begin in different places when it comes to their knowledge of the subject. One child's parents may have already spent a considerable number of hours working with him on learning the names of the letters, the sounds they make, print concepts, and so on. Another child will show up having never held a single book. We also understand that children may have different aptitudes for these subjects. Developing number sense seems to come naturally for some children in our classes, while others struggle. The COVID-19 pandemic, it would appear, has only served to widen some of these gaps. I hope I'm not telling you anything you don't already know. I also hope you understand that these things I am talking about only serve to signal where we start working with children. Children may arrive with different levels of prior knowledge or different aptitudes, but they can all improve in these subjects with effective instruction. This belief lies at the heart of our entire profession.

The exact same thing is true for behavior. Children will arrive in different places with their knowledge, skills, and abilities. Some will have spent loads of time talking to their parents about their feelings. They can identify their own feelings and the feelings of others. They have worked on breathing exercises and ways to calm themselves down. They self-monitor and self-regulate with ease. Other children may have a natural aptitude for such things. Some children can effectively self-regulate with no need for instruction on the subject and are a singular joy to teach. The COVID-19 pandemic has served to widen the gaps in this area as well. For every child who spent their lockdown time with an adult who could help them develop emotional and social competence, it feels like five or six spent their time in front of screens or fighting with older siblings for toys all day. Again, I suspect I am not telling you anything you do not already know. What I often see practitioners fail to fully grasp is that, while children may arrive with different levels of prior knowledge and skills or different aptitudes, they can all improve their ability to behave in a way that leads to success with effective instruction. We just need to start providing it.

We have to start teaching behavior with the same level of intentionality that we teach subjects such as literacy and math. We have to devote the time, tools, and curricula to this in the same way that we do those other subjects. Effective instruction begins with observing children. We might sit down with a child and have them count some objects to see what they can do. As they do so, we notice that the child is able to count the objects by assigning each one a single number, so they have developed one-to-one correspondence. But, when they finish, we ask them how many objects they have, and they tell us their favorite number, three, even though there were five objects. We understand that this child has not developed an understanding of cardinality (that the last number we count is the total number of objects).

This understanding informs our next steps. We explain the cardinal principle to the child, demonstrate how to use it ourselves, and then we do some guided practice in which we have the child count, and we scaffold their answers. Over time, we gradually fade out our support as they become better able to do the skill and apply their new knowledge independently. We will continue to monitor the child by observing their counting. As they continue to make errors or mistakes related to this, we will gently correct them and give them new opportunities to practice the skill. When they have developed a solid mastery of the cardinal principle, we will move on to the next skill (counting larger numbers). When they have mastered that skill, we will move on to the one after that (producing sets of objects).

Moreover, because this child is one of eighteen students in our class, we cannot possibly hope to remember where every single child is without some help. To that end, perhaps we have a table with the children's names down the side and the progression of skills across the top. We can then signal to ourselves where each child is on the counting trajectory. This lets us organize children for our small-group instruction and reminds us, when we push into the blocks center, exactly what each child there is working on. It lets us know, when we go to choose activities for tabletop time, which page of our curriculum to turn to for help.

Effective instruction in math is about more than just throwing spaghetti against the wall and seeing what sticks. It's not enough to put children in play-based centers that we know are developmentally appropriate and hope good things will happen. We have to take those developmentally appropriate centers and use our own knowledge of children's abilities and content to create situations that lead them to learn and practice those new skills. Perhaps, for our counting child, we move into the dramatic play center and help them set up a restaurant. Then, we play chef to their sous chef. When another child orders beans for their dinner, we give our sous chef a small number of beans and have them count them out for us so we serve the correct amount.

Learning, of course, extends beyond center time, so maybe we also have them count chairs at a table after cleanup is done to be sure we have the right amount. At lunch, we have them count the orange slices on their plate. I could go on, but I think you get the picture. In math, when we teach it optimally, we do it intentionally, and we layer instruction through the whole day.

The approach must be the same for behavior. Doing a ten-minute lesson during morning meeting about feelings is great, but it is not enough. Talking about procedures in the first six weeks of school is necessary but not sufficient. The children have shown us that this is simply not enough. They need more instruction and help in this domain. If we want to see changes in challenging behavior in our classrooms, it is not up to the children to figure it out. It is up to us to teach it.

HOW LONG?

Imagine, if you will, a two-year-old boy. Let's also pretend that you are a kindergarten teacher. (For those of you who are kindergarten teachers, this will be your easiest assignment of the day.) Let's imagine that this two-year-old's big brother comes home every afternoon and gets out a set of letter flash cards. He sits down with his little brother and starts reviewing the letter sounds: "This is the letter *A*. It makes the /n/ sound. This is the letter *B*. It makes the /sh/ sound. This is the letter *C*. It makes the /p/ sound."

Each day, that big brother comes home and teaches his little brother the wrong letter sounds. Every Monday, the little brother is learning that *A* makes the /n/ sound. On Fridays, the big brother is reinforcing that *B* makes the /sh/ sound. Even on weekends, they are going over how *C* makes the /p/ sound. Every single day while this child is two and then three and then four, they are reviewing these flash cards. Then, he shows up in your kindergarten class.

Here's the big question: How many days would it take you to teach this child the correct letter sounds. Is it one day? one week? one month? six weeks? Keep in mind that every night, when this child goes home from your class, his big brother gets out the flash cards and continues teaching him the wrong letter sounds.

When I do this exercise with teachers, they often recognize the difficulty here. They see that, for some children, it might take all year to correct these misconceptions. For other children, they might not leave their classrooms with all the correct letter sounds. Regardless of how long it takes, it will be a process. What you must understand—and some of you are sharp cookies who already see where I'm going—is that for many children, this is how behavior works. Remember those pesky maladaptive behavioral patterns? Some children have spent years developing them before they arrive in your classroom. Some of them are still having them reinforced every day when they go home. To unwind all of this will take time.

You will still have high expectations for each of the children. However, like a teacher who wants the children counting and producing sets up to thirty by the end of the year, you will also recognize that that is a goal rather than where children are at the moment. To get children there will require intentional time and effort.

This is important to understand not just because of how we approach teaching behavior but also because it affects how we feel stress. I am convinced that much of what stresses us out in this field is the gap between where we think children should be and where they are. This is true not just for where children are but also for their rate of progress. When I hear teachers say things like, "We have been in this class for six weeks. You should be able to do this by now," what they really mean is that their expectation of the rate of progress is higher than what children are doing.

I hope the preceding flash card exercise has helped you rethink this. If some children have made any measurable progress within the first six weeks, it's a blessing. It also makes it clear that, while we must approach behavior the same way that we approach any other subject we teach, the results are likely to come more slowly. Most children don't have siblings at home sabotaging your work in literacy or math. They certainly do when it comes to behavior. (To be clear, I'm using siblings as a metaphor here for all the different factors that lead to maladaptive behavioral patterns. This isn't the time for you to start a vendetta against the big brothers and sisters of your students. Please refrain from suggesting that their parents leave their older children in the woods like Hansel and Gretel, with nothing to eat but the homes of innocent old gingerbread manufacturers.) Part of teaching behavior is accounting for the fact that you may be swimming upstream with a significant portion of your class, meaning that additional patience and altered expectations for progress will stand you in good stead as you undertake this endeavor.

OUR PERCEPTION OF BEHAVIOR

I spend a goodly amount of time traveling about the country, helping states, districts, Head Start collaboratives, and sometimes even individual schools and centers figure out better ways to work with behavior they find challenging. This means that, sometimes, I will be away from home on a Friday afternoon with some time to kill before heading to the airport. Often, I will head over to the local Bennigan's or what have you to enjoy an early dinner. I often see, near the bar, a group of teachers. I know they're teachers because there are eight of them crowded around a single pub table, each with a glass of adult grape juice in front of them. Then, I'll see one of them shake her head and say in an exasperated tone, "Johnny," before rolling her eyes and taking a big drink. Before she says a word, I know exactly what it is about Johnny that has her out at a bar, drinking with her colleagues on a Friday afternoon. It's that Johnny is forgetting the number seven when counting objects. It could possibly be that he's mispronouncing the /th/ sound, but it's probably the seven thing. Right?

This is, of course, a joke. I have never, in all my twenty-five years in this field, seen or heard teachers out at a bar drinking because of children's challenges in traditional academic subjects. It's always about behavior. Challenging behavior raises our cortisol in a way that math and science and literacy simply do not. However, Johnny talking in the line or hitting a child to get a block or making fart noises during your whole group are all the same thing as him forgetting the seven or mispronouncing the /th/ sound.

All of these actions are indications that Johnny has not mastered a particular skill and needs scaffolding and guidance. Being prone to missing a number while counting does not make Johnny a bad person. Mispronouncing a phoneme does not mean that Johnny is out to destroy us. Making fart noises in whole group doesn't mean Johnny needs to spend time thinking about where he went wrong in his life. Rather, each of these instances represents information that Johnny is giving to us about his current skills and abilities. When we see him miss the seven, we make a note and begin to work with him on remembering that number. When we hear him say /v/ instead of /th/, we remind him to stick his tongue out between his teeth. When he makes a fart noise, we drink.

If we want to retain our sanity and reduce challenging behavior, we have to reframe the way we see behavior. We have to start treating it as we do all the other subjects. When we notice it, we see it for what it is—an indication that children are not yet where we want them to be. It is an invitation to help them move forward. Seeing challenging behavior this way is a powerful part of decreasing the stress we feel and recognizing our role in helping children become better humans by teaching them the things they need to know.

Before moving on, I want to confront a common misunderstanding that teachers take from this—that it means there are no consequences for children because we are just teaching them behavior like we teach anything else. None of what I said erases your responsibility to do job number one (safe bodies and happy hearts). Remember, job number one comes before, but does not replace, job number two (teaching children what they need to learn). Recognizing that Johnny needs to work on skills does not mean that Johnny is now functioning in a consequence-free environment. If he hits a child to get a block and this happens more than once, you may need to have Johnny participate in other centers until you or another adult can accompany him to the block center for some guided practice. Your primary responsibility is to keep those other children safe while you teach Johnny. Indeed, recognizing that Johnny needs to learn new behavior skills helps many teachers remain calm and collected while making the decisions they need to make to keep everyone safe, limiting the possibility that you will damage your relationship with Johnny or react in a way that is punitive rather than one that prioritizes physical and psychological safety.

THE CLUMP

I am hesitant to teach you what I am about to teach you. Of all the topics I have included in this book, this is probably the most polarizing. In the end, I have decided to leave this section in, not because I want you to adopt this practice necessarily, but because discussing it will illuminate some important concepts and ways of thinking.

I mentioned during my *Shawshank Redemption* story that I had been thinking about transitions and how much time they took up during my day. For me, the two biggest wastes of time were bathroom interruptions/stops and lining up. Even well into my teaching career, I was still pushing for an orderly line. I had let go of requiring children to have their hands in just the right places, but I was still requiring silence and for children to be standing on exactly the right tile before we would leave. This often resulted in us starting to line up, the children not meeting expectations, and us coming back to the carpet or our tables to try again. However, my data showed that far too much time was being spent on what I now recognize was a worthless endeavor.

Walking from place to place in an orderly line is, like quicksand, just not something I run into in adult life as often as I thought I would. As I reflected on how I could bring down my transition time, I decided to try something radical. I would no longer have my students walk in a line. Instead, we would walk in what I affectionately named "The Clump." On the first day we tried it, the new procedure went something like this: I would say, "Clump up!" Then, the children would get in a big clump by the door. I would say, "Go to lunch," and they would walk as quickly as possible to lunch in a big clump. As they got to the cafeteria, they would form a line as they went through the door.

If you are reading this and thinking what a horror show that sounds like, I want to take a moment to assure you that it was not that bad. If you are reading this and thinking, "What a wonderful solution to a difficult problem," I want to take a moment to assure you that it was not that good. As was the case with my Shawshank bathroom epiphany, I learned a lot that first time out. We ended up setting four boundaries to help us with our jobs.

First, we assigned a clump leader. Everyone in the class would have to stay behind the clump leader. I would position myself at the back of The Clump to sweep up stragglers and monitor everyone. Second, we decided that we needed to keep hands, feet, and bodies to ourselves. This prevented pushing and shoving, of course, but it also kept small hands and feet away from the walls.

Third, we decided that talking was okay as long as you did not activate your voice box. We had spent a lot of time already talking about voice box activation—when learning letter sounds, some have voice box on, and some have voice box off. (For example, the /b/ sound and /p/ sound are made using the same mouth motion, but /b/ has voice box on and /p/ has voice box off.) Talking with your voice box off is just whispering, but my students liked the connection to their literacy learning. At any rate, this decision to allow talking was intentional. Children need to talk to one another. Imagine spending a day at a professional learning event where you could not talk to your friends at all. You would probably quickly resort to texting, passing notes, or surreptitiously whispering. On the other hand, if you got frequent breaks during which you were allowed to chat, none of those previous communication strategies would be necessary. Allowing whispering permits children this outlet without disturbing other classes in the hall.

Our fourth boundary did not come up right away. There was an unfortunate incident involving my class mowing down a class of third graders.* After that, we decided that The Clump should stay on the right-hand side of the hall so we could keep the big kids safe.

I loved The Clump. Between The Clump and my new bathroom policy, I gained almost an hour of instructional time a day. This allowed me to spend more time working on project-based learning and providing individualized instruction to the children.

Many of the teachers with whom I have worked over the years love the idea of The Clump as well. In follow-up surveys from my talks, The Clump was one of the

---

* I shouldn't laugh, but the look of surprise on those nine-year-olds' faces is burned into my memory. They were so sure they were going to win that game of chicken. They. Did. Not.

most widely cited ideas that teachers were going to take back to their classrooms and try. Unfortunately, for states, districts, and centers where I was able to include a follow-up visit as part of my work, it was also most often cited as the thing that "didn't work," so I want to dig into The Clump a little bit to talk about why that is and what can be done to remedy the situation. In the process, I hope to help you more effectively use everything you learn in this book.

The biggest reason that The Clump did not work for practitioners who took it back to their classrooms is that we often treat professional learning as a buffet. We spend a day at a conference or spend a weekend reading a book, looking for one or two things that we can quickly pop into our own practice. At most, we are often replacing a single discrete practice by doing it in a different way. Teachers would do this with clumping. They would unplug lining up and plug in clumping. Unfortunately, many of the practices I include in this book are built on a certain way of viewing and understanding the behaviors that challenge us as adults. They are built on a certain way of seeing and understanding children and what they are about as well. When teachers try to implement discrete practices without bringing along the underlying framework, the results are often, at best, ineffective or, at worst, disastrous.

Here is how that plays out in The Clump. I view behavior as something children learn, just like anything else. To learn anything and do it well, we have to practice our new skills. Sometimes, practice means succeeding and sometimes it means failing. With three-, four-, and five-year-olds, it often means failing. However, the practice is important. What does failure look like when we are talking about self-regulating in the hall? Running, talking, pushing, shoving, touching the wall. If your lens on behavior is that it is a prerequisite to being a good member of a classroom community, and then you implement The Clump, you will be in trouble. All these behaviors that I just mentioned are more likely to happen in The Clump than in a line where you are controlling everything children do. To someone with this lens, using The Clump and seeing all these things happen would constitute failure.

Let's step back and consider my lens. I want children to practice self-regulation. I would prefer that they do not do it during instructional time, as that could distract from other learning (thus, preventing me from doing my second job). A straight line with children's voices turned off and hands in assigned places to be does not allow them to practice much at all. I have traded self-regulation for other-regulation. Children are more likely to get in front of the clump leader than the line leader.* Children are more likely to touch another person when there are four other children

* I blessedly was able to stop complaints about cutting as there is no cutting in a clump.

all around them. Children are more likely to slip up and talk when they're already whispering. But I never viewed these things as challenging behavior. Rather, as we discussed earlier, they are the behaviors of children who are learning but not yet proficient. Seeing these things occur did not raise my blood pressure. Instead, they gave me information. They told me who still needed to work on the behaviors. I would then move in to teach or scaffold or assist as needed. These are, after all, what we teachers do when we see a child trying to do something that they cannot quite do independently.

I sometimes get to speak with practitioners who have been using The Clump for years to great success. The teachers who brought The Clump back to their classrooms and had it work talk to me about its challenges. They talk about how the children struggle at the beginning of the year with so much freedom. They talk about how they spend the first few months of the year constantly monitoring and correcting while other teachers glide through the hallway with their quiet, pristine lines.

But they also talk about how they see the children slowly getting better. They talk about how, near the end of the year, their children whisper their way through the hallways, leaving them to focus on learning when they are in the classroom. Mostly, these teachers talk about how much extra time they have for the things that matter. The Clump, and lots of the other approaches we are talking about here and in the chapter on supporting children's autonomy, only work within this framework—this way of seeing behavior as just another thing to be taught.

GERMANS, FRENCH, AND THE PLASTIC PLATYPUS

In the early 1980s, just as I was taking my first steps, a French professor in Germany named Jean-Pol Martin began pioneering a new way to teach his students. He began having them take turns teaching each other French. This was not done in a haphazard way but rather quite intentionally. The teacher would provide initial instruction on a subject and then have students work in pairs or small groups to teach others what they had recently learned in whatever way they deemed fit. The teacher would circulate through the room, supporting and scaffolding as needed to ensure that all the students learned the material.

Like many school systems at that time, much of the emphasis was on conformity and rote learning.* Because of this, many German schools rejected this method of instruction. However, as is often the case, good ideas eventually proliferate, and now, *Lernen durch Lehren* ("learning by teaching"), or LdL as it is known in Germany, is a frequently used instructional technique in secondary and university settings.

Although research on LdL's effectiveness is mixed (Fung, 2019), there are numerous indications that some positive effects are to be gained from having children teach other children (Fiorella and Mayer, 2013). Specifically, while children who simply study a topic often have similar scores on tests to those who teach someone else the topic, when the follow-up examination is delayed, those who teach seem to retain the information more effectively. Because of this, I would routinely have my students instruct one another in behavior and procedures throughout the year.

At the beginning of the year, this would mean sometimes not establishing or reviewing procedures in a whole-group setting. Instead, I would choose a small group of children to work with while the other children were doing centers or an alternate activity. My small group would go to a center or part of the room, and we would have an in-depth discussion of what we wanted that center to be like so we could all do our jobs. We would then condense our discussion into three or four big ideas. Then, I would facilitate these four or five children in thinking how they wanted to communicate this to the rest of the class.

An important point here is that I *facilitated*. I didn't lead or provide the idea. I simply kept them on track. An important reason why this strategy of teaching as learning works is that it requires children to think about their thinking and forces them to remember what they just learned. They have to remember what we decided, then take what they know about these big ideas and imagine what might happen with them in different scenarios. Mostly, I am there to keep them from defaulting to just telling the big ideas, which is probably not the best way for anyone in the class to learn them.

Often, our teaching strategies included dramatic re-enactments. In particular, children relished the idea of making me pretend to be the child doing the wrong thing so they could correct and help me figure out what to do instead.** In the event that

* Before you criticize, I think it is important to keep in mind the purpose of schools when talking about things like this. At the time, many of the jobs individuals were being prepared for were either agricultural or in factories. Critical thinking was not the success indicator that it is today.

** Also, if I am being honest, I had so much practice being the "bad kid" in class when I was a child that this was effectively the role I was born to play.

important points did not come across during the group's explanation, I was there to fill in gaps to be sure that everyone got the big ideas.

Another way I helped the children teach one another behavior involved the child-selected rules. After their establishment, we would periodically review them to be sure that no new issues were cropping up and that everyone felt like the rules were still helping us do our jobs. When new wrinkles arose that we did not talk about at the beginning of the year, I would have children (often the one who recognized a problem) work together (often with the one who was causing the problem) to help everyone see how we might better understand the rule and ground it in how it was keeping us safe, happy, and learning.

This approach helped me maintain my hands-off approach to these rules but also gave children who had recently had a conflict an opportunity to partner with one another to teach a better way. I think that a particularly important part of why this worked so well for me was the children in my classroom—because of where they were in their cognitive development—often operated from a me-first perspective. Following up on a disagreement, incident, or pattern of behavior in this way allowed them to see how the conflict related to our broader classroom community and to see the perspective of the other person without either child having to be the bad guy. Because the children in conflict were united in their purpose to educate the rest of the class, they were able to see the issue without the emotional charge that dominated their views during the conflict and find ways to prevent its recurrence, a role for which they were uniquely suited given their recent engagement in said conflict.

This brings me to another factor that I think makes this such an effective tool: my intentional inclusion of the children who engaged in the most challenging behaviors. Often, in this approach, the person who learns the most is the child doing the teaching. Since the children with the most challenging behaviors need to learn the most, I always made sure that they were the ones teaching the most. When we first started doing this, the process could feel counterproductive because these children sometimes had enough difficulty self-regulating that they struggled to get through their conversations. The teaching sessions could feel like a chore. However, over time, as they saw themselves as experts on the rules, procedures, and jobs inherent in our classroom community, the process smoothed out and paid dividends in the form of fewer challenging behaviors outside the teaching sessions. The final thing I want to say about this concept is that, sometimes, I had children who were sufficiently dysregulated that participating with a group in this endeavor was simply not possible.* In those cases, I leaned on what is known as plastic platypus learning.

In plastic platypus learning, the idea is that we want the learner to teach an inanimate object (such as a plastic platypus) just as we would have them teach another child. This works because the interaction between the students is not what is important here. What is important is that we are requiring the teaching child to recall something and then act on that information, further cementing it in their knowledge framework (Koh, Lee, and Lim, 2018). Obviously, you don't have to use a plastic platypus.* Although the most sophisticated teachers often do. Any stuffed animal or toy will work fine. As a matter of practicality, I find that toys a child can assign a personality to, but that the child is not already attached to, work best.

TEACHING BEHAVIOR WITHIN THE FRAMEWORK

Children often arrive at our doors with all the motivation they need to behave in the way we want them to, but they often lack the ability to do so. As children get older and their brains develop, they will improve their ability to self-regulate. However, if we want to maintain our hairlines and our sanity, it is probably best if we give them a gentle push in the right direction. To do so, we have to take seriously the idea of teaching behavior. We have to provide instruction and deliberate practice with plenty of feedback in a supportive environment where failure is not only tolerated but encouraged. This process will take time.

* * *

For any particular skill or ability, when it comes to the children who are currently exhibiting the types of behaviors that challenge us as adults, we are looking at weeks or months rather than days in most cases. This makes teaching behavior something of a middle ground between supporting motivation, which is a lifetime endeavor, and our next topic, nudges. Regardless of the timeline, teaching behavior intentionally is necessary if we wish to see children at the end of the year acting in a different way than they acted at the beginning. However, if you are wondering what you can do tomorrow to reduce these challenging behaviors, the next chapter will be right up your alley.

* I also had times when I simply wanted to work one-on-one with a child, free from the distractions of other children.

CHAPTER 9: TASK DIFFICULTY

Choice Architecture in the Classroom

Just as no building lacks an architecture, so no choice lacks a context.

—RICHARD THALER,
NUDGE: IMPROVING DECISIONS ABOUT HEALTH, WEALTH, AND HAPPINESS

In chapter 4, we discussed my heuristic for understanding children's behavior in the classroom: Motivation + Ability = Task Performance. We have covered how we can affect children's motivation and their ability. Now, it's time to discuss how we affect task performance directly. We do this by changing the task difficulty of what we are asking children to do in the classroom. As we begin to think about this topic, I want to make sure we are on the same page about what I mean by a task. Some of you are likely imagining *task* with a narrow definition: a specific thing that I have asked a child to do, such as going into a center and writing a story about a unicorn named Barney Rumphauser fighting for good in a post-apocalyptic Australian outback. Such a thing would certainly fall under my definition of a task, but I am thinking about tasks more broadly. A task is anything we ask children to do in the classroom.

Some of these tasks are explicit and specific, like my unicorn example. However, others may not be explicitly stated each day. They can include things such as children will sit quietly on the carpet during circle time; children will keep their hands, feet, and bodies to themselves while lining up; and children will keep playground sand on or near the ground. Some of these tasks may be parts of rules that you discuss at the beginning of the year (for example, keep your friends safe) while others may be implied but never actually stated (for example, do not leave the class line to walk into the office and have a chat with the receptionist when we are on our way to music). Having a broad definition of what counts as a task is important, because it will allow you to see literally everything the children do in the classroom as consisting of one task or another. (We often have children engaging in multiple tasks simultaneously.)

In 2008, Richard Thaler and Cass Sunstein published the book *Nudge: Improving Decisions about Health, Wealth, and Happiness*. Thaler is a behavioral economist and recipient of a Nobel Prize in Economics, and Sunstein is a Harvard law professor who served as the White House Administrator of the Office of Information and Regulatory Affairs.* They are both A Big Deal™, and their theory has proved to be incredibly influential to both economists and politicians.

In short, nudges seek to remedy situations in which we act irrationally or not in our own best interests. The classic example of a well-used nudge has to do with retirement savings. Saving money for retirement is important, as most folks will not be able to make ends meet with Social Security alone. Most of us know this. Logically, we in the United States would then sign up for a 401(k), a 403(b), or a 457 plan offered by our employers. However, research on the topic suggests that only about

---

* Thaler looks like he should be the villain senator in a political thriller. Sunstein has a World Top 10 combover.

20 percent of employees do so within three months of starting work. The number grows to 65 percent within three years of employees' start dates, but that still means that a third of American workers are not taking advantage of these tax-advantaged retirement plans.* This kind of behavior is referred to by behavioral economists as *irrational behavior*. Nudges are small changes in the environment or procedures that help push people to do the right thing.

In the case of retirement plans, researchers asked some companies to begin automatically enrolling employees in a plan when they started work rather than requiring them to sign up (Madrian and Shea, 2001). Employees were free to check a box to opt out of the plan if they so wished. When this small shift was made in the onboarding procedure, 90 percent of new employees enrolled in a retirement plan. Within three years of their start date, the number rose to 98 percent. This is an enormous effect for such a small, simple change. Behavioral economists place nudges into three broad categories: decision information, decision structure, and decision assistance (Münscher, Vetter, and Scheuerle, 2016). Within these three broad categories are nine sub-categories. Many of these are not applicable in the classroom, so I won't bore you with their details. However, I find a few of them incredibly useful in shaping children's behavior so they can be the best versions of themselves. The specific sub-category that I use most is changing option-related effort, which is just a fancy way of saying make it easy to do the right thing and hard to do the wrong thing.

DEVELOPING THE PROPER ATTITUDE

Before we get too deep into applying choice architecture and how we use it to reduce challenging behavior in the classroom, I want to center us back on our roles as teachers and caregivers. Doing so will allow us to maximize our own motivation and sense of empowerment as we address task performance.

Back when I first started presenting on the topic of challenging behavior, I included a slide that simply said: **It's Your Fault.** I would then proceed to tell teachers that everything that happened in their classroom was their fault.** While I was presenting at a Michigan Association for the Education of Young Children conference, a teacher

* Many employers match what employees contribute up to a certain percentage, meaning that employees are further incentivized with free money, yet they often fail to sign up.

** Let the empowerment begin!

came up to me after my presentation concluded and said to me, "Hey, I really liked your presentation except for that one slide that said, 'It's your fault.' I feel like we're working in a profession where teachers are criminally underappreciated, the pay is lousy, and everything we do is increasingly difficult. It doesn't feel right that teachers are coming to a conference that's supposed to lift them up and being told that everything is their fault." I said, "You know what, you're right. How about we change that slide to say: **It's Your Responsibility.**"

She said, "I really like that. Thanks for listening to my feedback." So I did. Now, when I present to practitioners about challenging behavior, there's a slide that says, "It's Your Responsibility." But I want all of you reading my book to know and understand this: Everything that happens in your classroom is *your* fault. Every. Single. Thing. Is. Your. Fault. And I mean that in the most freeing and uplifting way possible.

Because here's the thing: I want you to think about Johnny, our caricature of a child who exhibits almost nonstop challenging behaviors. If all this challenging behavior is Johnny's parents' fault, can you go back in time and make them be better parents? No. If all this challenging behavior is because of Johnny's neurodivergent brain chemistry, can you write him a prescription or reach into his brain and rewire it so he can self-regulate like Suzie does? No. If all this challenging behavior is because of the full moon, can you reach into the sky and change the lunar cycle? Absolutely not. There is literally nothing you can do about any of these things, so if they are what is responsible for Johnny's challenging behavior, you will be unable to do a single thing about it today. However, if it turns out that Johnny's challenging behavior is *your* fault, then what can you do about it? That's right. You can do anything you want, because you are in charge of what happens in your classroom. Isn't that freeing? Isn't that empowering?

I once participated as a facilitator in a pre-K–3 reform project called FirstSchool. The purpose of our reform effort was to create a more seamless pre-K to third-grade experience in schools so children were no longer going from full-day play in preschool to sitting still on the carpet for three hours in kindergarten. At the end of our three-year project, we went on tours of all the participating schools with the leadership teams from each one. These teams included researchers like me, classroom teachers, principals, center directors, and even the district superintendents.

During our tour of one school, I was with two teachers from other schools, a principal from another district, and the superintendent of the district in which our tour school was located. We walked into a kindergarten classroom and stood next to the circa

1920s radiator to spend a few minutes watching what they were doing. The classroom was laid out like this:

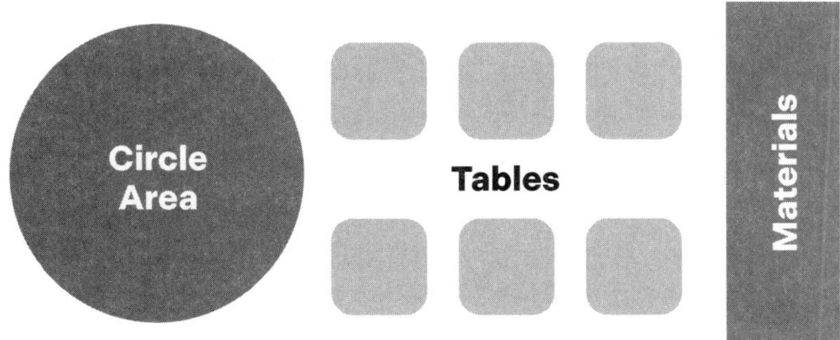

The teacher had all the children sitting on the carpet in the circle area, while we stood at what would be the bottom of this diagram watching. Within about ten seconds of walking into the classroom, I could already tell who this teacher's Johnny was. There's an item on the Conners scale (Conners, 1973), which we use to diagnose ADHD, that says, "Acts as if driven by a motor." That was this child. He was seemingly incapable of even a moment of stillness. It was also clear within moments of entering the room that this teacher was at the end of her rope with him. He stood up at one point while she was giving directions, prompting her to bark, "Johnny! This is your last warning. One more slip and I'll be sending you to the office!" The teacher then completed her directions, which indicated that the children would be using die-cut construction paper in the shape of pattern blocks (yellow hexagons, red trapezoids, green triangles, and so on) to create a pattern on strips of paper. The strips of paper would then be wrapped around their heads, and they would wear them as crowns during a parade that afternoon.

She then sent the children to their seats, where they waited for her to pass out the materials. She went quickly to the cabinet where she had everything divided out by table and then started placing them on the tables closest to the materials closet. Johnny, however, was at a table next to the circle area, and it was right as the teacher turned around to bring the materials to the second table that Johnny climbed atop his chair to get a better look at what she was doing. As soon as she spotted this, her face turned beet red and she completely lost it.

"That's it, Johnny! I told you that if you did one more thing to test my patience, you'd be going to the office." To make a long story shorter, it turns out that Johnny was not interested in going to the office. In the end, it took three adults from the office to literally carry Johnny, screaming, from the room. Johnny continued to scream so loudly as he went down the hall that, even with the classroom door closed, I heard the pitch change when he went around the corner at the end of the kindergarten wing.

I would be willing to wager that this teacher went home that night, poured herself a big glass of adult grape juice, and said to her husband, "You are not going to believe what Johnny did today."* She blamed Johnny. I know this because she wrote me and the rest of the observers a lengthy email detailing how responsibility for the aforementioned incident rested with a five-year-old. Having made it this far in the chapter, though, I suspect you know who I blamed. I blamed her.

I blamed her because I have shared this story with hundreds of groups, ranging from preservice teachers to experienced practitioners to district and state education leaders, and every time I have shared it, I ask those groups if this teacher could have done anything to prevent what happened. Now, I always give teachers the benefit of the doubt, so let us assume that the class was doing something at their tables before I ever walked into the room. Because they were engaged in another activity before we arrived, we will not suggest that the teacher could have had the materials on the table when she sent the children back. Even excepting this potential solution, I find that every group identifies at least two things the teacher could have done to prevent Johnny from ever ending up atop that chair. I'll give you a second to brainstorm a potential list. Got some possible solutions?

First, the teacher could have made Johnny her "special helper." He could have been right next to her, holding her hand, and assisting her in passing out the materials. Second, she could have started passing the materials out to Johnny's table first rather than saving it till the end. Either of these solutions would have likely resulted in a positive experience for the children, a positive experience for Johnny, and a positive experience for the teacher herself. If there is one thing I've learned after working in this field for twenty-five-plus years, it is this: Idle hands are the devil's tools. You should never leave Johnny alone for two minutes with nothing to do! If you do, you will surely reap what you sow, and you certainly should not be surprised when a bored five-year-old climbs up on a chair.

To come to the heart of the matter, let us go back to who is to blame for this. In this teacher's mind, Johnny was to blame. This means that she went home on Friday night, enjoyed her glass of wine in an attempt to block out the horror of the day, and then went back to school Monday, changing nothing about her practice. However, if she had blamed herself for what happened, she would have thought about what

* Keep in mind that the superintendent of her school district was in the room for this performance.

she could have done differently and almost immediately stumbled onto one of the solutions I shared a moment ago. Then, when she returned to the classroom on Monday, she would have done things differently in the future. That matters, as she would have effectively reduced the amount of challenging behavior in the classroom. Blaming yourself for the problems in your classroom, school, or center is certainly uncomfortable at first, but it is the only way we will ever grow into better practitioners.

DESIGNING A SMOOTH EXPERIENCE

This brings us back to task difficulty and how we leverage this to reduce challenging behavior in the classroom. Before we arrive there, I hope you will indulge me in one more brief aside that I think will lay the groundwork nicely for what we are about to discuss. I think we are at the point where we all realize that we should not be talking on our cell phones while we are driving. I live in a state where this has not been a point of emphasis for law enforcement, and I see roughly a quarter of all drivers on the road engaged in some way with their cell phones. I suspect that many of them think they are doing a good job of multitasking, but I want to assure you that they are sadly mistaken. They are generally speeding, driving too slowly, engaging in a fun mix of both, swerving, running stop lights, or missing their exits and swerving across the highway in an attempt to belatedly correct their mistake. I can practically hear some of you saying now, "But Dr. Holland, my state only allows hands-free, so I'm not doing any of these things." Unfortunately, even driving hands-free lowers your reaction time as much as if you had a blood alcohol level of .08 percent (National Safety Council, 2012).

We know we are not supposed to be talking on our phones, but when our wives/husbands/significant others/friends/offspring/dogs call, we almost can't help ourselves. We pick up the phone (because we know that if we don't pick up what they want at the grocery store on our way home, they are just going to make us turn around and go right back out to pick it up). This is the same issue that many children in our classrooms have. It's what psychologists call an issue of *inhibitory control*. Issues with inhibitory control arise when we know, consciously, that we shouldn't do something, but we do it anyway. In this case, we know we shouldn't answer the phone because it creates an unsafe situation, but we do it anyway. In our children's case, they know they shouldn't make fart sounds during our story time, but they do it anyway. It's the same failure for both of us.

I have a friend who never answers the phone when she is driving. She does not possess iron willpower. She is just the same as you and me. The way she prevents herself from doing so is with a little nudge. Instead of putting her phone in her pocket or in a holder on the dashboard, she puts it in the backseat in her purse. That way, when she is driving along and the phone rings, it is not right at hand. She is not *completely* preventing herself from answering the phone. Upon hearing it ring, she could undo her seatbelt, let Jesus take the wheel, climb into the backseat, get her phone out of her purse, climb back into the front seat, buckle up for safety, and answer the phone. She does not do that, however, because it's so much harder (and clearly more dangerous) than just reaching up to press a screen.

A few months ago, I was on my phone a bit too much (not in the car, just in life). I found myself picking up the phone, opening it, and beginning to type *f-a-c-e-b-o* until the browser auto-completed the web address, and then beginning to scroll, all without ever consciously making the decision to get on social media. When I stopped to think about it, this was a little terrifying, as it was compulsive. I would do it during meetings, while watching TV, while waiting in line at the grocery store, and even when playing with my son. Any time I became just a little bit bored, I would be, a few minutes later, scrolling Reddit or Instagram or Facebook without ever consciously deciding to do so. Tackling this issue involved a multilayered solution that I won't fully dive into here, but step one was simply placing my phone farther from my hand. When lying on the couch watching TV, I would place my phone across the room on a side table. When in line at the grocery store, I would button the pocket it was in. When playing with my son, I would put the phone on its charger in another room. At no point did I throw my phone away or turn it off or set restrictions on the device itself. However, this simple step of making it harder to start the process of using social media effectively reduced my use to almost zero.

The thing is, standing up and taking two steps or unbuttoning a pocket are trivially easy to do. However, adding the extra impediment gave me enough time to consider whether spending time mindlessly scrolling social media was what I wanted to do. (And 99.9 percent of the time, my answer has been no, even in the grocery store line.) In both cases, my friend and I have used choice architecture to do what I call *designing a smooth experience*. A smooth experience uses choice architecture to remove any potential cognitive or physical impediments to doing the right thing while making it just a little more difficult to do the wrong thing.

Sometimes, using this approach in the classroom means changing your environment and procedures to completely remove the possibility of the target behavior occurring.

Other times, we will simply create a little friction between a child and a behavior, knowing that this will not eliminate the behavior but will probably serve to reduce it to manageable levels. In still others, we will use choice architecture to increase the likelihood that children choose a replacement behavior. The approach we take will be dictated by many factors that will require our professional expertise, so let's talk about some examples and then some guidelines for which approach you might take. Let's use a common issue that pops up from time to time to illustrate how we might use each of these three strategies or even a combination of them.

THE WATER FOUNTAIN TEMPTATION

When I observe classes, challenging behavior seems common in the water line after recess. Children are playing, they line up, and they walk back into the building with their teacher. They stop at the water fountain in the hall or in the classroom. Each child takes a turn getting water. During this process, children are often still excited from being outside and have not calmed their bodies yet. This, paired with the boredom of waiting in line for water, can lead to challenging behavior. Children might poke at each other, start to play and get loud, or do any number of things that set adults on edge.

How might we design a smooth experience by completely removing the possibility of misbehavior in the water line? The easiest way to do this would be to get rid of the water line. In my own classroom, this was the route I took. Each child brought in a water bottle from home. After recess, the children would come in and get their water bottles and then take them to their rest spots or cots, which would be set up before we left for recess. They would refresh themselves alone in a dark room, precluding the possibility of the kinds of misbehavior I was used to seeing when we tried to get water in the hall.

Perhaps, for one reason or another, water bottles are not a possibility in your own classroom. How might we then reduce the issue in the water line without fully removing the water line? To do so, we need to think about the factors that promote challenging behavior. These factors may include elements from the environment, such as how children are positioned and the materials they have access to; what is going on, such as their state of mind, the overall energy of the class, the type of activity in which they are about to engage; and the functions of the challenging behaviors, meaning what children are trying to accomplish with their behaviors rather than just what they are doing to accomplish it—the why rather than the what.

In many cases, a key factor is not just the water line but proximity as well. When children are close together, they are more likely to have trouble exercising inhibitory control. Their limited willpower will not be up to the task of ignoring a temptation like their good friend standing two feet away with his finger up his nose. Therefore, the first thing we might do is separate the children. As with my phone, the distance does not need to be extreme. Just a few extra feet between each child in the line can make a significant difference.*

Another factor that promotes challenging behavior might be, as we alluded to already, *who* each child is next to in the line. Setting a full line order could solve this issue. You would simply set the order (who is first, second, third, and so on) intentionally, so that children most likely to play together do not stand next to one another. Being excited after recess could be still another factor leading to challenging behavior. Stopping your line briefly before entering the building to do some deep breathing or a brief meditation could bring heart rates, adrenaline, and cortisol all down to base levels, leading to calmer children in the water line. None of these solutions will completely eliminate challenging behavior, but they are all—particularly when used in combination—likely to reduce the incidence of challenging behavior to more manageable levels.

Finally, we could work to increase the likelihood that children choose a replacement behavior. Do you remember what we noted earlier about idle hands? My experience observing countless water lines is that idle hands are the predominant kind of hands in the water line. Engaging children just a little during this time serves to reduce challenging behaviors considerably. Some interesting strategies that I have seen teachers deploy in these situations include singing songs quietly, particularly ones with accompanying fingerplays, such as "Five Green and Speckled Frogs," practicing a dance, bringing a daily piece of artwork or artifact for the class to consider and discuss, allowing children to share something interesting they have done in or out of school, making plans for later in the school day, or even having a bit of a story time. Each of these strategies replaces the idle hands, which often choose to do the wrong thing, with busy hands and brains, which are more likely to do the right thing. These teachers have effectively designed a smooth experience for the children by providing

---

* Some of you are no doubt recognizing a weakness in this approach. Spacing children out means that a line of twenty children could stretch a significant distance. However, there are multiple ways to address this issue. You could put half the children on one side of the water fountain and the other half on the other, with yourself standing near the fountain. You could also split your class and put them on different sides of the hallway, thereby halving the length of your line. Great teaching is about maximizing benefits while minimizing costs.

them with an easy way to engage in the behaviors that they want rather than those they do not.

THINKING ABOUT OUR CHOICES

Now that we have seen how each of these approaches can work in a single situation, let's talk about how I make decisions about choice architecture. When should we eliminate the possibility altogether versus reducing the likelihood of challenging behavior versus making it easier to make the right choice? As I mentioned earlier, the decision may come down to hard-and-fast rules in your school or center (such as, all teachers are required to take their classes to the bathroom before dropping them off at music/PE/art/recess, or all children must be silent in the halls), decisions that you have made in the classroom (such as, morning circle time is an important part of building classroom community, so getting rid of it is not an option), or just personal preferences (maybe you hate fingerplays and refuse to incorporate them into your practice). These will put some clear boundaries on what you can or cannot do.

Once I have established those, I usually begin thinking of a list of approaches to try. As with the Shawshank Bathroom Incident of '07, not everything you try will be a winner at first. When I make my list, I always think first about how I might completely eliminate the challenging behavior. For example, if I have two children who have difficulty sitting next to one another on the carpet, I would try completely separating them during group times. I might put them in different groups or put them far away from one another without a direct eyeline between them, for example, before I tried something like putting extra space between them, which would only reduce the likelihood of challenging behavior.

When you have a few ideas, you should then think about what potential consequences you are introducing by changing your environment or procedures. For example, when I move the two children who cannot sit next to one another, I need to be mindful of where I am moving them *to,* not just where I am moving them *from.* (This is similar to our earlier situation, where we added space to the line and created a much longer line.) All this is to say that you will likely need to find ways to solve the problems created by your solution. In some cases, you may see issues that you cannot solve. You can then cross out those potential solutions. You may also see solutions that cause more problems than they solve. I also generally cross those out unless I am desperate. Let's run through one more example to illustrate the process.

Imagine that I teach a whole group writing lesson each day in my kindergarten class. As the year goes on, challenging behavior becomes a real problem during this instructional period. It occurs near the end of the day, so children are restless and have trouble focusing on me. Instead, they seem to be focusing on making fart noises and poking at each other. I have already assigned seating on the carpet so that children are generally sitting in rows next to someone that I do not envision them playing with during instruction. What could I do? Answering this question will require me to think about factors that promote challenging behavior in this situation, which might include:

- the time of day, when children have exhausted their ability to self-regulate;
- the size of the group—more children means more to manage;
- my ability to teach content in everyone's zone of proximal development (bored children are more likely to become distracted or seek other means of entertainment);
- the proximity of children to other children; and
- how much time children will need to self-regulate to get through the lesson.

To increase my odds of success, I will want to address as many of these factors as possible. I also should think about whether I can eliminate the behavior entirely. In this case, I am not sure I can. The only way to do so would be to remove the entire context. After my whole-group time, I include an opportunity for children to work individually on their writing. After they write, I conference with each child one-on-one. However, I think that the whole-group shared writing time is important. It gives the children an opportunity to learn from one another and for me as a teacher to introduce and demonstrate lots of different writing skills in a small time frame. This leaves me with the possibilities of promoting behaviors that I want to see and making it difficult to do the things I do not want to see. In addressing the factors I have listed, I will likely be doing both.

The first thing I consider is changing is the time of day. I could move my writing block to the morning. However, doing so would mean moving something from the morning to the afternoon, so there would be a new problem to solve: how to prevent the same misbehavior from occurring during that instructional block. Also, because children write at different rates, I have them transition to a snack time when they are done. It prevents me from worrying about children racing to finish writing to get to an enticing activity such as free-choice centers and, because their big mouths are full of food, the slow writers can generally finish in a quiet environment. In the end, I decide not to address this factor because the juice isn't worth the squeeze.

The next factor I consider is the group size. When we do classroom observations that include counts of challenging behavior, the most likely activity setting in which those challenging behaviors will occur is whole group. Therefore, having fewer children in the group could reduce challenging behavior. If I were by myself, I could have one set of children write independently while the other group does shared writing. Then I could switch the groups. However, I have an instructional assistant who is usually doing housekeeping tasks during this period. If I moved her task time to another part of the day, I could split the group into two and each of us could take half the class. This becomes an intriguing solution. Because my assistant and I meet one-on-one with each child daily, we know exactly what every child is working on each afternoon. Splitting my group would allow my assistant and me to focus more intensely on what each child needs during the shared group-writing time rather than using the spaghetti-against-the-wall method of instruction, where we try to teach lots of good things and hope that some of them stick. I love it when I can get two birds with one stone, so I decide that we will try this out.

Now, I need to solve the issues created by my new solution. I need a second area that can accommodate a lesson for half of my students. My assistant and I confer and decide that she will teach a lesson at the large whiteboard in the front of the class. I will teach children sitting at tables in the back of the room with a small whiteboard easel. We will meet twice a week to ensure we are aligning our shared writing lessons with the needs of the children in our groups. When we need to, we shuffle children from group to group so the focus is always on what each child needs. For example, if a child has been in one group working on hearing vowels in the middle of words, but this week's work will be on punctuation, which they have already mastered, we might move them to the other group.

I like this solution because it leverages two types of nudges. First, I am increasing the likelihood of seeing engaged behavior from the children by placing their instruction on exactly what they need each day. Second, I am decreasing the likelihood that they will play with friends during instructional time by halving the group size, which reduces the number of children who could distract them and places them physically closer to an adult. Huzzah!

Finally, I consider the proximity of children to one another. There are many ways we can have children sit on the carpet for group times. The three I see most often are haphazard, where children sit where they like, in rows, or in a circle. Haphazard seating gives children the most autonomy, and as we discussed earlier, providing children opportunities for autonomy is important. Sitting in rows does not give children as much autonomy to choose where they sit; nor does having them sit in a circle. Against the issue of autonomy, though, we need to place the issue of how easy it is to engage in challenging behavior in each setup.

While haphazard seating provides the most autonomy, it is clear from the issue we are trying to resolve that the amount of autonomy may be too much. I often find with haphazard seating that the transition can become challenging. Children may race to the carpet to get the best seats, losing control of their bodies in the process or neglecting necessary tasks in the prior activity (such as fully cleaning up their center).

Rows are often attractive to teachers because they take up less room than a full circle. However, again we must consider the opportunities for misbehavior. The issue with rows, specifically, is that each child is surrounded by eight other children. Even with assigned seating, it can be difficult to find nine children that can all sit around one another without any issues.

This leaves circles, which take up more room but place a maximum of two children next to each individual—a much more manageable situation than the one we saw in rows. To that end, I will be arranging the children in circles for both groups.

Finally, I must consider how long the lessons are taking. There is tremendous variance in how long children can sit, inactive, during a whole-group lesson. I like to think of three minutes multiplied by the child's age as a starting point. This means that, when I was teaching three-year-olds, I tried to keep any whole-group task under nine minutes. In kindergarten, I had a little more leeway and would try to keep whole group under fifteen minutes. These are just starting points, though. I strongly suspect that five-year-old Adam Holland, bursting with ADHD and boy energy, would not have been capable of sitting still for fifteen minutes. The children in my example here have been having similar troubles, leading to what I call plowing.* I resolve to shorten the shared writing part of the lesson by five minutes and increase my conferencing time by a similar amount.

This example tracks a real issue that I have worked through in my own practice and with multiple teachers. It nicely illustrates the power of a series of small nudges to shape challenging behavior in the classroom. I have yet to work through something like this with a teacher and have them fail to see real improvement. Often, incidences

---

* Plowing is what I call the tendency of teachers, when they have a certain amount of content to get through, to continue a lesson even when it is clear that the children have largely checked out. It can cause a lot of stress for teachers, who feel trapped and powerless as they try to finish up a lesson that, for the children, finished five minutes ago. As my son enjoys "singing" at max volume at 5:30 AM at least two mornings a week, you have to "Let It Go."

of challenging behavior are more than halved when employing such an approach, and best of all, this approach does not take weeks or months to put into place or see benefits. You can put it into place in your classroom tomorrow.

GLOBAL NUDGES

Before we wrap up thinking about nudges and how we can use them to change the difficulty of different tasks we ask children to do in our classrooms, I want to introduce a couple of more global nudges that you may find beneficial. These techniques are not focused on shaping the difficulty of an individual task but are commonly employed by behavioral economists and persuasion scientists who study things like marketing and donations.

First, as we have learned from *Inside Out 2*, we all have beliefs about ourselves with varying degrees of accuracy. These beliefs drive much of our behavior, as we generally wish to remain consistent with them. For example, if I believe that I am a good friend, and one of my friends asks me to help him move, I will probably help him if I am free to do so. The effect is even more pronounced when we advertise this belief to others. That is, if I tell my friend at a party that I am working hard on being a good friend, I am even more likely to help him move when he corners me later in the evening. We can use this to our advantage.

I believe that, as part of the classroom community that you create, it is important to include a statement that says, "We are all working on something." That is, after all, why children are in your classroom. Each child (and adult!) is there to learn and grow each day. The thing each of us is working on will be different. Some children are working on remembering what sound *W* makes. Others are learning how to share and take turns. Still others are practicing controlling their bodies when around other children. You will notice that, in addition to tying into classroom community, this also ties into teaching behavior. Many of the goals we have for children will be academic in nature, but just as many will be focused on their development in other domains.

Once we have established that everyone is working on something, the next step is to make explicit what each child is working on. You will be teaching many children many things, so do not overwhelm yourself or them by sharing with them every goal you have. Instead, focus first on easy wins. Give them a couple of options to choose from and then have them publicly commit to working on these goals. I used to literally have my students stand up during a morning meeting and say, "Today,

I'm working on ______."* These are discrete and easily achievable goals you set with a child. One such goal might be, Jazz keeps her hands and feet to herself while moving from the classroom to lunch. Now, when you notice that Jazz achieves her goal, it is worth taking a moment to pull her aside to remind her of her growth. You might say something like, "You are the kind of person who works very hard on learning and practicing new things. I noticed that you kept your hands and feet to yourself all the way through the hall and into the cafeteria. I appreciate that." This should be sincere appreciation. Children work so hard each day, and they are not perfect, but they are doing the best they can and deserve to have that hard work recognized by the adults they love. This statement, though, also serves the double purpose of cementing this belief within Jazz. Now, as she views herself as the kind of person who works hard to learn and practice new things, this belief will exert more influence over her behaviors. Nudges like this can be powerful.

I want to make sure that I offer a few additional pieces of information about this strategy, as I have seen it implemented poorly many times with unfortunate results. First, when you are lifting up and recognizing the child, focus on how hard they work. Do not focus on innate abilities.** Second, when you are building positive beliefs, you will want to focus on who that child is. However, when you are providing gentle corrections and feedback on times when Jazz maybe doesn't make it down the hall without kicking someone, you will want to focus on the action (for example, "Kicking is not a kind choice. Please choose to keep your feet to yourself, Jazz."). Critiquing the child—rather than the action—in this situation can do the opposite of what we want, cementing within her the idea that she is a bad kid or a kid who cannot control herself. Finally, I will note that this should not be a one-time thing. Rather, you should always be on the lookout for the small successes, so that you can build up your relationship and each child.

* * *

I hope that this chapter has given you something to think about. Challenging behavior is happening now, so approaches that require weeks or months to see change can be difficult to implement when we are just trying to keep our heads above water. Hopefully, our discussion on nudges here has given you some new approaches to try so that you can implement the levers that will lead to longer-term, more lasting changes. In the next chapter, we will turn our sights to integrating our three approaches, seeing how they work together to reduce challenging behavior now and in the future.

---

* Public commitment to something is a powerful nudge that falls under the decision-assistance category.

** You will remember that this is an important part of supporting a growth mindset.

CHAPTER 10: GOOD HABITS

Building Relationships One Interaction at a Time

The only proper way to eliminate bad habits is to replace them with good ones.

—JEROME HINES,
AMERICAN OPERA SINGER

So, I've spent much of this book trying to convince you that kindness and relationships matter more than the rewards we offer or the punishments we threaten. Hopefully, you have found these arguments convincing and are ready to make some changes to your practice. The good news is that this is the first step in becoming a better practitioner. The bad news, unfortunately, is that this is easier said than done.

In a perfect world, intention would translate perfectly to action. That is, if I decide that I want to be kinder to the children in my class, I would then need only to go out and do it. Unfortunately, as anyone who has ever taken up a New Year's resolution or started a new diet knows, intentions can be more difficult to act upon that it would first appear. Psychologists estimate that between 40 and 90 percent of our behaviors throughout any given day are the result not of well-thought-out actions but of habits (Walesh, 2017). In general, this notion of habits taking up so much of our lives is helpful. It allows us to go through the motions of our day without wasting precious cognitive resources thinking through the mundane tasks we consistently do. Imagine if every time you went to pour a bowl of cereal or start your car, you had to think about it. You would be exhausted. I often think of habits as little robotic cleaning tools (like a Roomba) that largely work on autopilot so we can focus on the good stuff.

Knowing that habits have this particular function, I think it will come as no surprise to you that we tend to use habits more at some times than at others. Stress and distraction reduce our motivation to consciously pursue goals, leaving us to fall back on habits (Petty, 1996). Again, that can actually be adaptive. Even when we are in these sort of non-optimal situations, we have a baseline level of competence that we will likely be able to demonstrate.

The flip side of the coin, however, is that changing habits can be quite challenging, which brings us back to the classroom. We would like to think that each thing we do throughout the day is intentional and well thought out. However, you will remember that the *baseline estimate* of how much we do out of habit is 40 percent. Now, think about what I said about stress and distraction. Have you ever been stressed out in the classroom? distracted? Good! Glad to know it isn't just me. I would argue that managing a classroom is quite a bit more stressful than the average person's daily existence and presents slightly higher numbers of distractions as well. Taking this into account, I would hazard a guess that *at least* half of our classroom day is driven by habits rather than intentionally planned responses and behaviors. In some cases, that's good. Habits allow us to be quick and efficient in dealing with transitions, passing out materials, reading stories, and any number of other things. However, sometimes we develop "bad" habits, and it's overcoming these that can be the real barrier between our best intentions and best practices.

HOW HABITS FORM

Before we get to increasing good habits and ridding ourselves of bad habits, I think it can be helpful to think about how habits form and why bad habits occur in the first place. Let's use the cereal-making example to help us think through this. First, we gather our materials. We get a box of cereal, milk, a spoon, and a bowl. We pour our cereal into the bowl. We put an appropriate amount of milk in the bowl. We begin to eat.* The first time we ever set out to make cereal and we have assembled the ingredients, we have the potential to do any number of things. We could pour the cereal onto the floor and roll around in it. We could brush our hair with the spoon. We could drop-kick the bowl across the room. But we don't do these things. We pour the cereal into the bowl. When we take this action, our brain connects the actions together. Now, in our brains, pouring cereal into the bowl is connected to getting out the materials. With repetition, the connection between these two activities becomes stronger and the connection between assembling the materials and other possible actions gets weaker. Eventually, our brain connects these activities so strongly that we don't even have to think about them. We can make cereal while thinking about how we're going to get Johnny to line up to go to music, even though Johnny hates music class. The encoding of the habit sequence decreases the likelihood that we will choose alternative options, such as brushing our hair with the spoon.

Again, I hope you can see the upside here. By increasing our brain's connection from one activity to the next, we create a habit sequence in which we don't have to think about every step. Instead, our brain is freed to consider the weighty problem of Johnny's music hatred. The downside of this is that once we have a habit set up in our brains, it can be incredibly hard to change it.

If we want to use the fancy terminology that psychologists who study habits use, we can call the first action in the sequence the *cue*. The cue is the event that starts the ball rolling on the rest of the habit chain. Some cues are internal while others are external. For many of us in the classroom, our cues come from interactions of students with us and around us. For a long time, if I had sent my class to get ready

---

* Yes, I know that there is a small percentage of the population who put milk into the bowl first, but I'm writing this book for people, not monsters.

on the carpet, and I saw a student who was sitting improperly or talking to someone when they should have been silent, it immediately served as a cue to start a praising habit I had developed. I would scan my eyes over the group, find a child sitting properly, and say, "I *like* the way Emily is sitting silently, criss-cross applesauce, with her hands in her lap!"

Funnily enough, this was my hardest habit to break. When I started to change my own practices in the classroom, I took down my card chart immediately. That ruled out my other most used response, "So-and-so, go flip your card," but with the praise thing, there was nothing stopping me and so my brain just defaulted to it. It literally took me months to get away from it. In the end, I had to slowly detox. I started by changing my habit to *noticing* children doing the right thing: "I notice that Cruz is sitting quietly, ready to learn" replaced *liking* things.* Eventually, I was able to stop noticing and only praise when I sincerely had someone to thank for something, but it was a real struggle. My brain just kept defaulting to what it had done so many times before.**

Researchers call the connection chain that we develop *automaticity* (Gardner, 2012). I like that term, because it highlights both the good and the bad side of habits. It's great that we can do tasks automatically, without wasting a ton of thought on them. It's also terrible that we do so many tasks automatically and can't consciously change them when we want to. So, where does that leave us? Well, it sort of depends.

CHANGING HABITS

I want to talk about two different kinds of habit changes. In the first kind, we have some level of control over the cue or the cue is fairly stable. For example, we may want to greet children at the door each day when they arrive so that they know they are valued, and we can start the day by making a positive connection with them. The start of the day has a stable cue: a bell,*** so we can build a new habit around that

---

* I do not believe, in spite of what many people think, that *noticing* and *liking* do anything differently in children's brains. Whether children are being noticed or praised, their brains interpret the words as positive regard from a trusted source.

** I also think it's worth noting here that rewards, whether they are natural consequences or artificial ones, serve to reinforce these habit loops. I hope you see that, even though it may seem like the students are the only ones being rewarded here, that is not true. When I praised my students, and twenty other students suddenly did what I wanted, that was a reward for *me*. It served to reinforce and cement the habit loop in a particularly strong way, as it was a natural consequence of my action.

*** Like with Pavlov's dogs.

stable cue. Other habits arise in response to unstable cues or cues that we have no control over. For example, the way I respond to a child tugging on my sleeve may be driven by habit. When and how—or even whether—a child tugs on my sleeve can vary completely from day to day. Because the cue is constantly shifting, changing that habit can be more difficult. (But often these habits are the ones we need to change the most!) So let's talk about each of these types of habits separately.

CHANGING HABITS WITH A STABLE CUE

First, let's talk about changing habits with a stable cue or a cue within our control. I lump these two together because, if the cue is within our control, we can make it stable. A good example for me is flossing. I floss when I get out of the shower. I don't necessarily shower at the same time every day, but I shower every day. That means that I also floss every day. Because the cue is within my control, I can make sure that it's a daily activity rather than a sporadic one.*

Back in the classroom, we can use cues within our control that happen daily to do any number of good things for our students. We can start a morning meeting after arrival time ends instead of just jumping into the day. We can greet children at the door and say a special goodbye in the afternoon. We can have special lunches with the teacher. Even if we are not naturally doing these things now, it's not too challenging to add them because the cues for them tend to be stable parts of our schedules. So, in the morning, I hear the opening bell or an alarm I set to indicate the beginning of arrival time, and I go to the door to greet children and families. At first, this requires conscious thought. I have made a decision to greet, so I decide to go to the door. Over time, the new habit routine will achieve greater automaticity while the old habit routine of running around the classroom, trying to accomplish last minute tasks, will become less automatic. Eventually, I won't have to think about it. My brain will just automatically lead me to the door of my classroom when the bell goes off.

It's certainly possible to initiate a number of changes at once using this method, but I prefer to go slowly and steadily. I will make one change and get it to stick. Then, I can make another change and get it to stick. By moving one change at a time, I'm using the automatic nature of habits to my advantage. That is, as habits become ingrained, I no longer have to think about them. As they become automatic, I can add new

---

* To be honest, I find showers to be my favorite cue to attach habits to in my personal life. At this point, my post-shower routine has grown to include a number of activities that have nothing to do with showering, ranging from meditating to taking a French lesson. Because showering is so regular for me, I attach a lot of steps to the end of it when I am trying to cultivate new habits.

routines or habits to my day without adding any stress or extra thinking. That makes for a nice, smooth transition.

CHANGING HABITS OUT OF OUR CONTROL

Now, I mentioned that cues within our control differ from those out of our control. Using our example from earlier, a cue that is out of our control might be when we are trying to do something and a child comes up, grabs onto our sleeve, and starts talking to us. This is sort of a classic example of when habits take over. We're stressed out and distracted in this moment, so we generally go to our default behavior. That default behavior probably has served some purpose in the past. (Often, the purpose it served is to get rid of the child so we can get back to our task.) As such, it has been repeated and become automatic. For a few teachers, the behavior is a positive one, but for many of us, that default behavior is mild sarcasm, eye rolling, or a sternly worded warning to "ask three, then me."

If this were a cue that we could control, we would place it at a more opportune time. We would have children come ask us questions when everything in the classroom is running smoothly and we're not stressed out, trying to accomplish ten things at once. However, we don't control this cue, and that makes this something of a sticky wicket when it comes to changing our habit. There are a few different ways to attack this issue, and I try to make use of multiple tools at once.

First, we can seek to change the cue. Here, the cue is initiated by a child, so it's somewhat out of our control, but it's not totally out of our control. After all, we are teachers. We can teach children new routines. In this case, how the cue changes isn't critical. What matters the most is that the cue is new, so instead of defaulting to our automatic, old habit, we can pave the way for a brave, new habit. How the cue changes isn't critical, but if we're in control here, we might as well make this work in our favor. Change the cue to something that is less likely to trigger a negative reaction and more likely to trigger a positive one, on the off chance that we aren't able to respond intentionally every time. Once the cue is changed, you can start setting up a sequence of behaviors that is more positive than the old sequence. For example, if I changed the cue from a child pulling on my sleeve and saying, "Mr. Hollaaaaaaaand," to a child standing right in front of me with their tongue out and their hand on their head, it will be a reminder to start my new chain of behaviors: I take a deep breath, get down on the child's level, and ask them how I can help them. What's nice about this is that, even if the child messes it up, I'm still in good shape. If they tug on my sleeve (because of their own bad habits), I can start by reminding them of the new cue we're using. Once they get in the correct position, I can start my new behavior chain.

I love this method, because even when they mess up the new procedure, I am still safeguarded to some degree against my old habits.

My second strategy for addressing bad habits goes deeper, and I'm going to pull from James Clear's (2022) popular book *Atomic Habits,* although the work underlying this technique draws from behavioral economics and the study of persuasion as well (Cialdini, 1993). In the last chapter, we talked about using a powerful tool of helping children define what they do as part of their identities and then drawing their attention to their own learning and development of these good behaviors. The same is true for us as professionals. Just as we can help children shape their identities and, by extension, their behaviors, we can do the same for ourselves.

In discussing habits, Clear talks about how many of us start with a goal in mind, such as I want to quit smoking. Then, we take steps to pursue that goal. Our behavior is informed by the external goal, which then shapes our identity. However, we could do the reverse. We could decide to be a different person. Clear provides an example of a smoker refusing a cigarette in two different ways. In one case, someone offers a cigarette to a person trying to quit, and the person says, "No, thanks, I'm trying to quit." In another example, the person who has decided to quit smoking is offered a cigarette and says, "No, thanks, I don't smoke." The second response flows from this new identity, aligning with—rather than pursuing—an external goal.

Even though I have visited this way of tying identity to behavior many times over the years, in various contexts, Clear's example struck me as powerful. In much the same way that Becky Bailey empowers teachers by proposing that no one can make them feel any way they do not want to feel, this example reveals the power we have to shape who we are on the deepest levels of our selves.

To go back to my own experience that I shared when talking about nudges, I was, at one point, A Person Who Consumes Too Much Social Media. When I decided to stop feeling out of control and spend my time on more valuable pursuits, I became A Person Who Does Not Consume Social Media. This new belief about myself, in combination with the nudges I employed to help me avoid unconscious action, was a powerful force in shaping my new habits. I would sometimes be standing in line at the grocery store, bored, and think about getting my phone out. However, mid-reach, I would then think to myself, "I'm not a person who consumes social media," and I would move my hand back to the handle of my shopping cart.

Let's look at how this is changing my habit loop. Before, the moment I would feel bored, I would reach for my phone to begin distracting myself from the boredom.

Every time I did this, I would further cement the habit; so, when I felt a similar boredom while writing a journal article at my desk, I would also reach for my phone to begin distracting myself. The habit made it hard to get work done, as my reaction to boredom became an immediate desire to relieve that boredom by playing with my phone. Now, because I am A Person Who Does Not Consume Social Media, I have also taken on a related identity: I am A Person Who is Comfortable Being Bored. When I am writing an article and I experience that moment of boredom, I think to myself, "This is okay. I am A Person Who Is Comfortable Being Bored." Then, I continue writing instead of doing something less valuable.

Each time I resist picking up my phone, it further cements my new identity. My mind is constantly pulled to notice all the times I succeed. I hope some of you are thinking critically about this. Maybe you are wondering, "But Adam, what if we slip? What if we say that we are A Person Who Doesn't Eat Sugary Sweets in the Office, but then Bill turns forty-one and Milton passes me a piece of cake and I eat it?!?" This is an important point, because it is incredibly rare for us to begin a habit wherein we don't ever fail or slip up. The important piece here is to not let this undermine your new identity.

Nobody is perfect, so if you lose your temper when a child pulls on your sleeve, it does not mean that you are suddenly A Teacher Who Loses Their Cool All the Time. You are A Patient Teacher Who Remains on an Even Keel who did a single out-of-character thing. Apologize to the child. Remind yourself of who you are. Forgive yourself. Take any steps you can to nudge yourself out of repeating the mistake, and then look for opportunities in the near future to do better. Find a child who is having a tough moment or exhibiting a challenging behavior and proactively go into the situation to help them with all your mental energy focused on aligning with who you are now. This will restart your positive feedback loop, allowing your identity to dictate your behavior and your behavior to reinforce your new identity.

WHICH HABITS ARE WORTH CULTIVATING?

Back when I was working on the FirstSchool project (the same one that led me into that Michigan classroom that we talked about in chapter 9), I had the pleasure of working in a small school in rural North Carolina that featured one of the best teachers (we will call her Stephanie) I have ever seen. One day, I was videotaping in her classroom, since the project wanted to get some video of best practices.

When I do this, I always have one eye on what we are looking for on the project and another open to try to figure out what makes a teacher great. It is often surprisingly hard to pin down, as I find that what separates good teachers from great ones is not a cataclysmic, transcendent moment. The heavens don't open up and illuminate the teacher with an otherworldly light. Instead, what makes teachers truly great is often a fleeting thing, captured in just a single moment during your limited time in that classroom. It makes them great because, although it is just a moment for you, it is evidence of a different way of doing things that permeates everything those children experience during their year in that community. On this particular day, I was fortunate enough to observe this fleeting moment and recognize it for what it was. I have thought about it almost constantly since then.

To set the scene (and I have watched it hundreds of times on video): Stephanie has divided her students into pairs and has allowed them to choose a place around the room to work on a math problem. She instructs the pairs to work together to solve the problem. She tells them that, when they are done, they can play or chat in the space where they chose to work, but she asks them not to move around the room, as that might distract the other children. I turn my camera toward her as she begins working with a pair of children at a kidney table over on the side of the room. She carefully works through the problem with the two children, and they explain how they solved it. They even tell her the strategy they used to deduce that the problem included unnecessary information. Stephanie's face lights up.*

Then, Stephanie looks up, behind where I am standing with the camera, and sees Tony out of his spot. Her expression clouds and the smile drops off her face.** I point this out because you can literally see it in the video: the moment when her cortisol level shoots up and her body tenses. It turns out that Stephanie is no different than you or me. She has the same stress response that we have. What matters, of course, is not how she feels. It's how she treats Tony in that moment.

She opens her mouth and asks, "Tony, do you need some help?" Tony replies that he's looking for a tissue. Stephanie says she will go find him one.

It's so innocuous. The whole scene that I laid out here takes ten seconds. It is, however, the difference between being a regular teacher and being one of the best teachers I have ever seen operate in a classroom. Let's break it down.

---

* We all know this feeling. It's the feeling that you get when you've been working for days or weeks on a topic and, all of a sudden, the kids finally *get it*.

** We all know this feeling. It's the feeling you get when you see Tony failing to follow directions for the twentieth time that day.

In most classrooms I visit, when the teacher looks up and sees a child out of his seat, they feel that rush of cortisol, they tense up, and they react, almost without thinking (out of habit):

"Tony, sit down!"

"Tony, move your clip!"

"Tony, you're getting a bad report home today!"

Often, poor Tony will attempt to stammer out his need in spite of this: "But, but, I just need ..."

All too frequently, such attempts only lead to more recriminations and frustration from the teacher, who is now upset that her latest set of directions are not being followed.

"I *said* go sit down!"

"If you want to talk back, you can move your clip twice."

"Keep talking, and I'll have even more to tell your parents!"

Think about it, though. Tony is just trying to take care of a basic need. He has snot sliding down his face, and he's trying to remedy the situation in the best way he knows how. Everyone I watch this video with agrees that he is doing nothing wrong here. The instruction to stay in their places does not mean stay in place no matter what. If a venomous snake got loose in the classroom, no teacher would say to the fleeing students, "I said stay in your places!" The instruction means stay in your place unless there's a good reason to leave it, and Tony has a good reason.

What does it do to our relationship with children when we react with frustration and punishments? The change is small, almost imperceptible, but it creates just the tiniest bit of separation. This reaction, however, is a habit, so it is repeated over and over and over with the Johnnys and Tonys in our classrooms. Each time, the separation grows just a little bit, but it adds up. By the end of year, Johnnys just know that they hate being in this classroom. After a couple years of this, they know that they hate being in school. Before you know it, they're starting clubs to overthrow their teachers.

That's not what happens here, though. Stephanie sees Tony out of his seat, doing the wrong thing. Her cortisol level jumps up. Her chest tightens and her mouth creases momentarily into a frown. Then, in a calm voice, she says, "Tony, do you need some help?" What does that signal to Tony? It reveals to Tony how Stephanie sees her own role toward him. She is there, not to teach a set of skills or knowledge, or to have everything go exactly the way she wants it to, but to *help him*.

This moment, such a tiny thing tells Tony everything he needs to know about Stephanie and their relationship. When we know someone loves us and cares about us, what would we not do for them? This two-second slice of Tony's life serves to move him and Stephanie just that tiny bit closer together. Because this is Stephanie, this is a habit, so it is repeated over and over and over with the Johnnys and Tonys in her classroom. Each time, their relationship becomes closer, just a little bit, but it adds up. By the end of the year, Tonys just know that Stephanie loves them and wants to help them. Having spent three years in Stephanie's class, I can tell you that the result of all this was that her classroom ran like a well-oiled machine. Tonys and Johnnys make mistakes, of course. They're only eight-year-olds, after all, but those mistakes vanish under a sea of earnest attempts by each child to do the right thing.

At its heart, this is about Stephanie's identity. She is A Teacher Who Helps Children. Because she is A Teacher Who Helps Children, when she is working with a pair of students and sees Tony doing the wrong thing, her first reaction, even under stress, is to ask how she can help him.

* * *

We should absolutely greet children at the door every morning and tell them how happy we are to see them. We should tell them we love them as we hug them before their parents come to pick them up. We should do the rituals that show how much we care. But, all of these things are so easily undone if we exhibit bad habits throughout the rest of the day. As we discussed in the chapter 4, the negative interactions can so easily overwhelm those positive ones. It's time to start thinking about how we approach the routine interactions with our children, the thousand times a day that we react rather than thinking through what we really want to say. None of us has the mental bandwidth to be intentional about all these things, so we have to rely on our habits. When we see that child out of his seat and wandering the room, will our habits cause us to say, "Get back in your seat!" or will they cause us to ask, "Do you need some help?" Only you can decide.

CHAPTER 11: GETTING BETTER

Never Enough Time

Work expands to fill available time for its completion.

—C. N. PARKINSON,
BRITISH NAVAL HISTORIAN AND AUTHOR

The previous quote is known as Parkinson's Law. I probably think about it more than most people do. It's not my Roman Empire or anything.* I just think about how I spend my time more than most people I know. I didn't learn about Parkinson's Law until after I had completed my PhD, but I certainly wish I had known about it while I was teaching. In this chapter, we are going to talk about how you apply the ideas you have learned in this book; that is, how you improve as a teacher. Throughout, we will largely be relying on the same theories and ideas that you have already learned about through the other chapters, but I want to use Parkinson's Law to frame it.

I'm going to rely on Parkinson's Law because the most common reason I hear from teachers about why they cannot do X or Y is that they don't have enough time. Parkinson's Law, however, suggests something different. Whether we are talking about being in school or being at work, teaching or being a middle manager at a Fortune 500 company, Parkinson's Law still holds true. We will never feel like we have enough time. For example, one of my project teams at UNC has reports, tools, and other things that we create for states and school systems throughout the year. We have never, in my fifteen years working at the university, turned a project in a month early. We have also never turned a project in a month late. This has remained true even when timelines have drastically shifted, such as something was originally due in December but our partners at a state department of education decided they needed it in November. Somehow, the project was still completed a month ahead of the original due date. All of this leads to a sort of frenetic energy around getting things done. We always feel like we are on the cusp of not quite fulfilling all our commitments. And yet, we always do.

When I taught, I felt the same pressure. The teachers I am privileged to work with each year often indicate the same. They feel like they don't have enough time to do all the things they want to do with children. They feel like they don't have enough time to do all the things they are called to do outside the classroom. Parkinson's Law gives us the reason. The amount of work we have will always expand to fill the time we have.

When I first learned about Parkinson's Law, I was pretty bummed. I had always thought that the feelings I had of always having more to do were something that I could escape. "One day," I told myself, "it won't be like this." But it always is. However, the longer I spend with Parkinson's Law, the more comfortable I have become with it. More importantly, the longer I have spent with Parkinson's Law, the more I have been able to bend it to my will. You see, if our work expands to fill our

---

* That would be clay-colored cars. Go ahead, Google "my Roman Empire."

available time, that means that our work does not overflow our available time. As I told you earlier, my projects never complete deliverables early, but they also never complete them late.

Before we understand Parkinson's Law, we often fall prey to prioritizing urgent, unimportant tasks over their less urgent, important counterparts. Knowing that my work will fill the time I allot for it allows me to take control of it rather than allowing it to control me. For us to apply what we have learned in this book, we must first take control.

In psychology, we call this idea of being in control *agency*. Our perception of agency in our lives is called our *locus of control* (Ryan and Deci, 2000). Some of us have an internal locus of control, which means that we believe that we are in control of what happens around us. Others have an external locus of control, which means that things external to us are in control of what happens around us. Take a moment to think about your day-to-day work in our field. You probably feel an internal locus of control sometimes and an external locus of control other times. However, researchers find that, over time, people tend to develop a predominant lean toward one or the other.

Many teachers I work with show me through their words and actions that they have an external locus of control. They say things like, "My principal won't let us do X," or "I wish I could do Y, but we just don't have time." These statements indicate an external locus of control. Somebody or something outside the teacher is constraining them and forcing them to do things. On the other hand, some teachers maintain an internal locus of control. They make statements like, "We've never done literacy like that, but I'm going to figure out a way to make it work," or "Hmm, that's an interesting idea. Can you help me rearrange my schedule so we can do that?" These statements show that these individuals believe themselves to be in control of what happens around them. Often, these two teachers work in the same school, so I know that it's not any actual difference in the level of control their school district or administrator are applying. It's in their perception of agency.

There are, of course, times when one really is or isn't in control. However, it turns out that our situations are more malleable than we often recognize. I know this because research is clear that people with an internal locus of control tend to exert more agency in their lives while those with an external locus of control exert less (Ryan and Deci, 2000). That makes sense if you think about it. People who believe they have the power to shape the world around them will do so. People who believe that the world around them shapes them will allow things to happen, even if they are not what they would choose.

Coming back to Parkinson's Law, we know that the work we have allotted will fill the time we have available. This means that we can let that time fill up, as we often do, with the "have-tos" that others put on us. Or, we could acknowledge that everything will get done in its time and be intentional about what we prioritize and do first. This is the key to unlocking our potential as educators. As we manage our time, we have to prioritize the tasks that are important and then fill in our remaining time with urgent but unimportant tasks.

FULFILLING OUR OWN NEEDS: AUTONOMY

Just as children have universal psychological needs, so do we. Because we are adults with the ability to make choices in our lives, we can (and should) be intentional about those choices. Rather than expecting our environment to fulfill our needs, we should ensure that our needs are fulfilled.

Let's start with autonomy, as we have already touched upon it in the opening to this chapter. My advice to you about autonomy will, of course, depend on your existing feelings about your own agency. So, I'd like you to take a moment to think about how much control you have in your life, particularly your work life. Each day, do you arrive at school feeling like the decisions you make lead to the outcomes you desire? Do you have control within your classroom? during your prep time? in meetings? Go ahead and rate, from one to ten, where you feel you are with regard to autonomy. It is unlikely that you will be either a one or a ten. Even if you are required to teach from standardized curricula, you probably get to decide things like how you want the children to sit on the carpet. Conversely, even if you have complete control within your classroom, you probably have to attend district- or state-mandated trainings from time to time.

Whatever your number is, I want you to think about how (not whether) you can increase your autonomy in one area of your professional life. Could you try something new in your classroom that you previously felt like you couldn't? If your time after school is not yours to do with as you will, could you come in ten minutes earlier in the morning to meditate before you begin your prep? Even if you are sitting at a level two, there is something small you can do to take control of your professional life.

Once you decide what that something is, I want you to commit to doing it five times. Perhaps that means every day next week. Maybe that means every Wednesday for the next five weeks. The time frame is not important, nor is the possibility that you miss a day or week. If you commit to coming in early five days, but you oversleep on Wednesday, that is fine. You will just extend your fifth day to be the following Monday. Missing one day is not a problem as long as it does not lead you to lose track of your commitment to fulfill your need for autonomy.

Why are we doing this? Because agency begets agency. As we slowly spread our influence on the world, our brain sees this and changes its beliefs about what we can accomplish. In the past, you may have thought to do something only to have your brain reply, "We can't do that." However, with every action you take that shows you do have agency, your brain's beliefs will slowly realign, allowing you to take even more control of your life.

I want you to supercharge this process by focusing intentionally on your autonomous actions. Educational psychologist Daniel Willingham describes memory as "the residue of thought" (Willingham, 2021). What we think intentionally about we are more likely to remember, as our brain strengthens the neural pathways that encode and retrieve that thought. By thinking clearly about our intent to be autonomous and then being autonomous, we are ensuring that our brain will easily access those memories of autonomy.

Similarly, I want you to reinforce your identity as an autonomous person. Habits guru James Clear (2022) talks frequently about the power of identity in shaping our habits and thoughts. By thinking about and describing yourself as an autonomous person, you align what you are doing with who you are as a person. As we discussed in chapter 10, there is a big difference between a recovering smoker responding to the offer of a cigarette by saying, "No, thanks, I'm trying to quit," versus saying, "No, thanks, I don't smoke." The recovering smoker who sees themselves as a nonsmoker is reinforcing their identity as a nonsmoker in words, thoughts, and actions, creating alignment within themselves. To that end, if you have always felt yourself to have an internal locus of control, reinforce that. If you have had an external locus of control prior to reading this, it's time to start thinking of yourself as someone who has made a change and is taking control of their life. By strengthening your identity, thoughts, and actions, you will find that the autonomy you seek is within your grasp.

FULFILLING OUR OWN NEEDS: RELATEDNESS

With autonomy taken care of, let's turn our attention to our need for relatedness. There are many ways you can fulfill your need for relatedness in an educational context. Let's start with the low-hanging fruit. You spend all day, five days a week, with a group of children. I have spoken at length in this book about how to form strong relationships with these children. I have also spoken at length about how to create a classroom community that is supportive and aligned in its goals. I want you to recognize that these connections you are building are basic human connections. Just as they fulfill the children's need for relatedness, so too will they fulfill yours. The need for relatedness is not about one kind of relationship. Rather, it encompasses many kinds of love and affection, including the kinds of love that we as teachers and caregivers have for the children in our care.

To supercharge this connection process, I want you to take just a few minutes each day to reflect on these relationships. Set a timer on your phone or watch to go off a few minutes after the last child has left each day. Clear all the distractions away and spend those three to five minutes just remembering the things that connected you to the children during your time together. These can be little moments of shared joy, or they can be situations where you got through a tough time. They can involve children with whom you had a one-on-one connection at some point during the day, or they can involve something that occurred with your classroom community as a whole.

I recognize that there will be days when you feel like nothing went well and you feel disconnected from your children, either individually or as a whole. That is okay, and it is completely natural to feel that way. This will come as a shock to a great many of you, but children can be real butts sometimes. In the event that this occurs, it is time to start thinking about repair. How will you fix the relationships that were damaged during a difficult day. If you have anything to apologize for, visualize how you will do so the next day you see that child or group of children. If you need to talk to the children about something that hurt your feelings or upset you, think about what you want to say, when you want to say it, and how you want that conversation to go. Think about how you can frame it to build on children's growth and learning. Think how good you will feel as your relationships become stronger after your shared struggle. The outcome of your talk the next day will not be that the children never frustrate you again, but it will be one more plank in the community that you are building within your classroom.

We often wish that we could avoid negative emotions such as anger, fear, or sadness. However, these feelings are important as they drive us to become better and to recognize when things in our world need adjustment. What is important when we feel these emotions, especially at the end of the day,* is that we figure out how we will handle what happened and then move past those feelings rather than allowing them to occupy our thoughts in our personal time. If you find yourself thinking about them later in the day or the next morning, just remind yourself that you have already created a plan and then move on to something else.

Finally, let us turn our attention to our own competence, which will have us revisit some of our past thinking on topics such as mindset and deliberate practice.

YOUR GROWTH MINDSET

In just the same way that children have a mindset about abilities, so too do you (Dweck, 2006). Your students have mindsets about math, reading, and even their general intelligence. As we discussed alongside our thinking about math and tennis, these beliefs are domain specific. You also have beliefs about math and tennis, but I want us to turn our attention now to your beliefs about teaching.

In many of my classroom observations over the years, I was there to collect data for the purpose of coaching teachers or engaging in an inquiry process. That is to say, I wasn't there to assign a star rating to their center or collect information that would be shared with anyone's bosses. It was about as low stakes as it could possibly be. Still, the way teachers treated those observations and the subsequent look at their data during our coaching session told me a lot about how those teachers viewed something like teaching ability.

You will remember that individuals with a fixed mindset believe that an ability cannot be changed. Some people "have it" and some people don't. Individuals with such a mindset often focus on outcomes as indicators of that ability. During something like a classroom observation, they would be intent on looking good or at least not looking bad. When I observe teachers who have a fixed mindset about teaching ability, their sweet students often are the first to let me know.

---

* See our discussion of colonoscopies in chapter 5.

As I sit in the back of the classroom, iPad or clipboard in hand, collecting my data, children near me will delight in the fun activity that the teacher is telling them they are about to do. Their little faces will light up. Then, overcome by excitement, they'll turn their wide-eyed gaze toward me and whisper, "We never get to do stuff like this!"

It's all I can do to keep it professional and not laugh out loud. What these children are telling me, in their charmingly naive way, is that their teacher is showing off. The practitioner or practitioners in the room aren't concerned about getting accurate feedback that could help them grow their practice. They are concerned with getting a good "score" on their observation, even if such a score has little to do with what they would receive on a "normal" day with their class. The focus is on looking good and getting a good score as that is what will indicate to themselves and others that they have a high level of teaching ability.

The way teachers react to the data and scores themselves is a giveaway as well, particularly if things did not go perfectly during my observation. When confronted with a score or piece of information that might suggest anything less than perfect teaching, they look me dead in the eye and say, "Well, you know I have Johnny, so what can I do?" or "I do believe that it was a full moon on the day you were with us." These are, of course, just examples. What shows me that they have a fixed mindset is that they are engaging in what I think of as ego protection. That is, they are assigning the blame for anything negative to factors beyond their control. Because the reason for the less-than-perfect score has nothing to do with them or their teaching ability, they can continue to believe that they have high ability, even if their score would indicate otherwise.

As you know from reading chapter 9, I believe that everything that happens in our classrooms is our fault, so I don't worry about the lunar cycle or the Johnnys. The issue for these teachers, however, is that this mindset is actively preventing them from becoming more competent. They don't see the negatives in their observation or data as being about them, so they don't change or improve.

On the other hand, when I sit down to review data with teachers who have a growth mindset, they see the same flaws and make comments like, "I wonder what we could do to improve my transitions," or, "I don't feel like I have a good handle on how to have children collaborate in math, so what do you think we could do to improve that?" As psychologist Brené Brown (2015) has noted, vulnerability is a key feature of individuals who wish to learn and grow. Therefore, becoming more competent as a practitioner requires us to be vulnerable about our practice.

For me, this starts by acknowledging that we are not our practice. As adults, we often do this. We see what we do and our mission at work as inherently part of ourselves, as part of our personalities. I have been out of the classroom for fifteen years now, but I still see myself as a teacher. This sort of alignment can make it easy to think that our teaching practice is part of who we are. It isn't. I might be a teacher, but my teaching practice is not me. It is something that I do.

Seeing your practice as external to yourself allows you to avoid the pitfalls of believing that critiques of it are critiques of you as a person. Instead, you can see it as something to be molded and changed as you see fit. Admitting mistakes still requires vulnerability, but it doesn't require feeling like you need to justify your deepest self. As Maya Angelou said, "Do the best you can until you know better. Then, when you know better, do better."

This is the heart of developing a growth mindset around your teaching practice. You begin with a recognition that your practice is not perfect. There are aspects of it that could be better. Some of these are things you already know about, and others are blind spots, places where you may think you are perfect but that others may see as opportunities for growth.*

Having a growth mindset is the foundation of improving your competence. It allows you to see more clearly where you can change and improve, and it provides the motivation and beliefs that will drive you to make those changes and improvements. It is a necessary but insufficient ingredient to fulfilling your need for competence. If becoming a phenomenal teacher were as easy as developing the proper mindset, we would have a much stronger education system than we currently do. To truly unlock your potential, you will need to push yourself beyond where you are comfortable and engage in deliberate practice.

DELIBERATE PRACTICE

In chapter 8, we talked about the "10,000 hour rule" and how children's improvement of their behavior requires deliberate practice. It requires spending real time pushing themselves beyond what they can currently do, with consistent feedback and coaching, to get better. The same is true for us.

---

* I am not asking you to blindly change everything that a classroom observer or coach brings your way. Sometimes, observers and tools have their own misconceptions or biases. However, it is always worth thinking about and reflecting on the feedback of others, even if your initial reaction is to reject it.

As we think about deliberate practice (Ericsson, 2008), I want to highlight that word *deliberate*. It means intentional or purposeful. Many of the teachers with whom I have worked think about all of their teaching practice as deliberate practice. However, this is not what researchers mean when they talk about deliberate practice. There is, of course, some built-in degree of feedback in our day-to-day teaching. If we try out a new way of teaching children to count objects, and they get bored within three minutes of the lesson starting, they will let us know with their actions. However, I would liken this again to going to a driving range and hitting golf balls. If we go by ourselves, the ball will give us feedback. If it slices off to the left or the right, we know we've done something wrong. The trick to improving involves knowing what we did wrong and how to fix it. This is not always as obvious as we would like (on the driving range or in the classroom).

To get better requires real work, when the children are there and when they aren't. To improve consistently, you will need to systematize your deliberate practice. This requires extra time and effort beyond what you have already committed to your job.

Still there? You haven't walked away in frustration and anger? Good, because I get that this is a heavy lift. Teaching is hard. Really hard. I've worked in construction (in the summer, in the South), at restaurants (front of the house, back of the house, manager), at a major state university, in a law firm, and in the acquisitions department of a library. None of these other jobs can hold a candle to how difficult teaching in the classroom is. So if you read that previous paragraph and said, "Ain't nobody got time for that," I understand.

However, I want to ask you to try, because I believe that in the long run it will make you happier and less stressed. Imagine that five days a week, two people are asked to lift a heavy weight each morning. Lifting the weight is exhausting. Each day, the two individuals risk injury as they pick up their loads and carry them. They arrive home exhausted. One of individuals says, "This is all I can do. When I'm not carrying this load, I'm going to rest." The other individual says, "If I keep carrying this load like this, one day, I'm going to hurt myself." The second individual then acquires a gym membership and a personal trainer. On the weekends, the second individual trains and works to get stronger. In the short term, the second individual is even more exhausted than the first. However, over time, the second individual gets stronger and stronger. After a year, they find the weight they are asked to carry five days a week to be lighter than it once was. This person traded short-term discomfort for long-term ease.

That is what I am asking you to do here in your professional life. In the short term, putting in additional time and effort is absolutely going to be difficult. It will require discipline and extra work. However, as you grow as a professional and get better at what you do, you will become more competent. Doing so will make your job easier in the long term and will lead you to feel more intrinsically motivated to teach.

BEGIN WITH VIDEO

If you're interested in possibly trading some short-term heavy lifting for a career that is easier, let's start thinking about what that entails.* The first place I will send you is to the video camera on your phone or tablet. Before we can engage in any kind of deliberate practice, we have to find ways to gain feedback. That starts with seeing what it is really like when you teach.

Aside from the fact that I hate my voice when I hear it on a recording, regularly watching myself teach was eye-opening. Often, when we are herding the cats while juggling on our unicycles, we think we look, sound, and act one way. However, video often shows us differently. Speaking for myself, I found that I was often more severe-sounding than I intended to be.

So for the next two weeks, I want you to videotape yourself for ten minutes working with children, twice a week. This could be in centers or whole group, inside or outside. Then, the same day you film yourself, I want you to watch the videos. For these four videos, you don't need to critique them. You don't need to purposefully look for anything. You just need to watch the videos to see what you look like when you are with children and to learn how to set your camera phone up effectively.* Depending on the layout of your space, you may be able to set the phone on a shelf with something propping it up, or you may need something like a tripod. After watching a few videos, you should have a good feel for whether you need to invest a few dollars in something to hold your phone.

GATHER YOUR TEAM

After taking a few videos and watching them, it's time to find partners in crime. You can choose to work with one teacher (or paraprofessional) or with a small group of three or four. They can teach the same age group you do or a different one. They can work in your school or center, or they can work elsewhere. These details are less important than finding other teachers who are committed to growth as professionals.

---

* I have adapted this method from Daniel Willingham's (2021) approach, which is featured in his amazing book *Why Don't Students Like School?*

You also want to find professionals with whom you feel psychologically safe—that is, people around whom you are comfortable making mistakes. This way, you know that they will see them in the context of you improving rather than seeing them as problems.

Once you have assembled your team, spend a few meetings watching videos of other teachers together.* You can find plenty of teacher videos on YouTube or on sites related to teaching and education.

After watching a video with your partner(s), you will then critique it. The point of critiquing videos that are not of any of you is that you can practice critiquing.** As you critique, you want to ensure that you are supportive. This means including positive comments. It can sometimes feel like this is fake, and it might even be a little fake. However, things like gratitude journals are equally contrived, but research suggests that this contrivance does not matter (Davis et al., 2016). Drawing our attention to the positive tends to uplift us and make us feel a greater sense of well-being, regardless of whether it is required or spontaneous.

Your critiques, however, need not only be positive to be supportive. What matters when you offer opportunities for growth or improvement is that your criticisms are offered in a way that makes it clear to the one being critiqued that your goal in doing so is to help them grow and improve rather than to tear them down. As you work with your partners to critique the videos of teachers who are not in the room, help each other monitor your tone, your focus, and your wording to ensure that the critiques you offer are truly supportive.

Second, in addition to being supportive, your critiques should be as concrete as possible. That means being specific, but it also means avoiding making judgments in broad terms and avoiding inference when possible. Rather than saying, "This teacher is really good," you want to share observations like, "Her clear directions anticipated challenges her students would have in this center, and that looks like they led to children knowing exactly what to do when they arrived there." Sticking to more concrete critiques will help you avoid making assumptions and potentially missing important parts of the context in a video. It will also help the person receiving

---

* I strongly recommend choosing a time to meet each week that you put on your calendars. I also recommend choosing a predetermined backup time in case something comes up during your originally scheduled meeting block. The goal here is to skip weeks as rarely as possible, because this can lead to losing the habit.

** If this feels like Deliberate Practice *Inception*, that's because it is. I love director Christopher Nolan, and practicing how to practice makes perfecting perfection perfect.

feedback target what they are doing because they will hear exactly how their words and actions affect their instruction. Furthermore, hearing criticism can trigger us to feel attacked personally, even if we logically know the criticism is meant to help us. Criticism targeted at actions and what is visible can help us avoid this feeling when it is our turn in the hot seat.

SCREEN TIME

The next step is to start videotaping ourselves and watching the videos with our partner or team. Unless there is a pressing reason to use longer videos, I like using a rule that videos are ten minutes or less so that you don't unduly burden your fellow teachers and vice versa. As you watch the videos, take notes (including on your own videos). As you did in the previous step, try to note some positive things. Whether you are offering positive or negative critiques, try to keep them grounded in what you see; make them concrete.

When it is your turn to give or receive criticism, Harvard happiness researcher Arthur Brooks (2024) offers four tips to maximize the chance that you and your partners will internalize the criticism in productive ways. First, he suggests receiving the critiques in a way that helps you remember that they are not personal. His own mantra, which he says before receiving a critique is, "I don't care what this feedback says about the person giving it, and I choose not to see it as a personal attack on me. I will assess it on its face about the matter at hand—nothing more, nothing less." Reminding ourselves of this right before hearing criticism can orient our minds away from an emotional response and toward a more analytic one, reducing the likelihood that we reject the criticism and instead incorporate it into our practice.

Second, Brooks suggests treating criticism as insider information. That is, it represents how people who care about you see you. By creating a partnership focused on improvement, we have already taken steps to create such a mindset. It never hurts, however, to remind ourselves of this fact as we convene and begin our work.

Third, focus on making and receiving your critiques as gifts, not weapons. Focusing on supportive critiques goes a long way toward making this happen. Just as you monitored your tone and words during your practice, you should continue to do so as you critique one another's videos. I often find it helpful, while taking notes during the video watching, to flag critiques that require some care in their delivery. After the video, I may think about these critiques and how they might be heard before delivering them. Doing so allows me to phrase them in such a way that they can be interpreted in the positive way that I mean them rather than as attacks.

Finally, Brooks recommends that we praise in public and criticize in private. For our purposes, this means a Las Vegas–style treatment of what is shared with others: What happens in this learning community stays in this learning community. Short of mandatory reporting, nothing that another teacher shares with you needs to go beyond the bounds of the group. Treating information this way will help everyone to be open about their shortcomings and struggles, a necessary step for improvement.

The last thing I will share about the video review sessions is that you will often be tempted to jump immediately from sharing what you see to offering solutions. You should only share solutions when they are asked for by your partner(s). When we share what we notice, we are a collaborative partner. As soon as we begin sharing solutions, it is easy to slip into the role of expert, which creates a different type of power balance between you. In the long term, this can be poisonous to your group. Therefore, you should avoid unsolicited advice, even if you are quite sure that your solution is brilliant and workable. When people are ready to hear solutions, they will ask for them. Until then, write them down in your special diary and keep them close to your cold, dead heart.

IMPLEMENT CHANGES

Once you have concluded your video-watching session, the real fun begins. Now, it is time to come back to the classroom and make changes. I have offered several helpful lenses in this book that you might use to find solutions to your challenges. Could you design a smooth experience to shift behaviors right now? Do you need to spend some time intentionally teaching behavior? Are there unmet needs that the children are exhibiting, which you could find ways to meet before they resort to maladaptive behavioral patterns? The only way you will find out is to try.

Even if your solution does not work and instead leads to children doing worse in the short term, you will have learned valuable information. You can then use that information to try other approaches. If you have trouble figuring out what is going on or how to approach the situation next, bring it back to the group. (Some of them have many solutions already written down in their special diaries.)

Each month, as your group works to improve, I find it to be valuable to check in and see how things are going. As with your video critiques, it is important to be honest with your colleagues and to hear their words in the supportive way they are meant. If you feel uncomfortable about part of the process, want someone to lean in or lean out, or need additional supports, this is the time to discuss them as a group. By checking in regularly, you can keep resentments from festering and ensure that everyone is getting something valuable from your time together.

* * *

In this chapter, I have tried to provide a road map for you on your journey toward addressing challenging behavior. To do so will not be easy, but it is not the insurmountable mountain that many of us feel like it is. I have tried to help you see how many of the theories and frameworks we have used to understand children can also help you understand yourself and your colleagues. If, at the end of all this discussion, some of the approaches I have recommended still feel like too tall an order, I would encourage you to do something, even if it means starting small. If getting a group of folks together is beyond you right now, grab your phone and record a ten-minute video just to watch it yourself. If making big changes to your procedures is too much, make a small change just for the one child who needs it. Once you do so and find a little success, it will be easier to continue moving forward. To paraphrase author Brandon Sanderson (2017), the most important step a person can take is always the next one. If you keep moving forward, progress will occur, and your professional life will move ever closer to becoming the one you have always wanted.

AFTERWORD

I hope you have found this book to be helpful. Writing it has truly been a labor of love, distilling many of the lessons I have learned from my own practice and from the practitioners in the thousands of classrooms that I have had the pleasure of visiting during my twenty-five years in this field. Whether you are a teacher, a parent, or someone who supports those who work with children, there are two key ideas to take from this book.

First, our attitudes about challenging behavior are often a bit askew. They prevent us from truly understanding children and why they act as they do. Moreover, they prevent us from responding in ways that will serve to reduce our stress and effectively manage complex situations. My experience in working with educators is that we often rush to do things, change things, and fix things. These are important steps, but implementing many of the changes I discuss in this book will only work if they are preceded by changes in your perspective. To that end, it is probably worth spending some time with your thoughts and feelings as you reflect on what you have learned. Examining them closely will allow you to better understand yourself and what you hope to accomplish in the classroom. Understanding yourself and the children will provide a firm foundation for what comes next.

Just as psychologists like Ryan and Deci were correct in stating that we can never truly understand behavior without understanding people's thoughts and feelings, so too was Skinner correct when he asserted that behavior is still of the utmost importance. If you read this book, put it on your shelf, and make no changes to your practice because of it, then reading it was a waste of your time and writing it was a waste of mine.* For you to begin reducing your stress, taking control of your practice, and giving the children what they need, you will have to make some changes. With the final chapter as a guide, I wish you luck as you begin making those changes. Keep in mind that while the challenges may increase in the short term, in the long term, you are laying the groundwork for a lifetime of success. How far you go is up to you.

---

* I'm not sure how you would feel about this situation, but it would be a bummer for me. I'm the most intelligent, handsome, humble person I know, and I consider my time to be valuable, so let's agree not to waste it.

REFERENCES AND RECOMMENDED READING

Ambady, Nalini, et al. 2002. "Surgeons' Tone of Voice: A Clue to Malpractice History." *Surgery* 132(1): 5–9. https://doi.org/10.1067/msy.2002.124733

American Heart Association News. 2018. "Are Eggs Good for You or Not?" www.heart.org. https://www.heart.org/en/news/2018/08/15/are-eggs-good-for-you-or-not

Bailey, Becky. 2015. *Conscious Discipline: Building Resilient Classrooms*. Loving Guidance.

Beckman, Howard B., Kathryn M. Markakis, and Anthony L. Suchman. 1994. "The Doctor-Patient Relationship and Malpractice: Lessons from Plaintiff Depositions." *Internal Medicine* 154(12): 1365–1370. https://doi:10.1001/archinte.1994.00420120093010

Benson, Kyle. 2017. "The Magic Relationship Ratio, According to Science." The Gottman Institute. https://www.gottman.com/blog/the-magic-relationship-ratio-according-science/

Brooks, Arthur C. 2024. "How to Take—and Give—Criticism Well." *The Atlantic*. https://www.theatlantic.com/ideas/archive/2024/06/criticism-happiness-wellbeing-defensiveness/678647/

Brown, Brené. 2015. *Daring Greatly: How the Courage to be Vulnerable Transforms the Way We Live, Love, Parent, and Lead*. Penguin Publishing.

Cialdini, Robert B. 1993. *Influence: The Psychology of Persuasion*. William Morrow.

Clear, James. 2022. *Atomic Habits: An Easy and Proven Way to Build Good Habits and Break Bad Ones.* Penguin Random House.

Conners, C. Keith. 1973. "Rating Scales for Use in Drug Studies with Children." *Pharmacotherapy of Children* [Special Issue]: 24–84.

Darabont, Frank, dir. 1994. *The Shawshank Redemption.* Castle Rock Entertainment.

Davis, Don E., et al. 2016. "Thankful for the Little Things: A Meta-Analysis of Gratitude Interventions." *Journal of Counseling Psychology* 63(1): 20–31.

Deci, Edward L., and Richard M. Ryan. 1985. *Intrinsic Motivation and Self-determination in Human Behavior*. Plenum.

Dragoi, Valentin, and J. E. R. Staddon. 1999. "The Dynamics of Operant Conditioning." *Psychological Review* 106(1): 20–61.

Dweck, Carol S. 2006. *Mindset: The New Psychology of Success*. Penguin Random House.

Ericsson, K. Anders. 2008. "Deliberate Practice and Acquisition of Expert Performance." *Academic Emergency Medicine* 15(11): 988–994. https://doi.org/10.1111/j.1553-2712.2008.00227.x

Ericsson, K. Anders, Ralf Th. Krampe, and Clements Tesch-Römer. 1993. "The Role of Deliberate Practice in the Acquisition of Expert Performance." *Psychological Review* 100(3): 363–406.

Fiorella, Logan, and Richard E. Mayer. 2013. "The Relative Benefits of Learning by Teaching and Teaching Expectancy." *Contemporary Educational Psychology* 28(4): 281–288. https://doi.org/10.1016/j.cedpsych.2013.06.001

Fung, Chak Him. 2019. "Stop Using Learning-by-Teaching. A Simple Revision Could Provide Similar Efficiency: A Case Study on Metacognitive Benefits." *Education Sciences and Psychology* 51(1): 3–11.

Gardner, Benjamin. 2012. "Habits as Automaticity, not Frequency." *The European Health Psychologist* 14(2): 32–36.

Gladwell, Malcolm. 2005. *Blink: The Power of Thinking without Thinking.* Little, Brown and Company.

Gladwell, Malcolm. 2008. *Outliers: The Story of Success*. Boston: Little, Brown and Company.

Gottman, John M. 1991. "Predicting the Longitudinal Course of Marriages." *Journal of Marital and Family Therapy* 17(1): 3–7.

Heyman, James, and Dan Ariely. 2004. "Effort for Payment: A Tale of Two Markets." *Psychological Science* 15(11): 787–793. https://doi.org/10.1111/j.0956-7976.2004.00757.x

Holland, Adam. 2013. "Children's Social Competence Across the Transition to Kindergarten: A Latent Growth Curve Analysis." PhD diss. University of North Carolina at Chapel Hill.

Koh, Aloysius Wel Lun, Sze Chi Lee, and Stephen Wee Hun Lim. 2018. "The Learning Benefits of Teaching: A Retrieval Practice Hypothesis." *Applied Cognitive Psychology* 32(3): 401–410. https://doi.org/10.1002/acp.3410

Langer, Ellen, Arthur Blank, and Benzion Chanowitz. 1978. "The Mindlessness of Ostensibly Thoughtful Action: The Role of 'Placebic' Information in Interpersonal Interaction." *Journal of Personality and Social Psychology* 36(6): 635–642. https://psycnet.apa.org/doi/10.1037/0022-3514.36.6.635

Lillard, Angeline S., et al. 2013. "The Impact of Pretend Play on Children's Development: A Review of the Evidence." *Psychological Bulletin* 139(1): 1–34. https://doi.org/10.1037/a0029321

Madrian, Brigitte C., and Dennis F. Shea. 2001. "The Power of Suggestion: Inertia in 401(k) Participation and Savings Behavior." *Quarterly Journal of Economics* 116 (2001): 1149–1225.

Münscher, Robert, Max Vetter, and Thomas Scheuerle. 2016. "A Review and Taxonomy of Choice Architecture Techniques." *Journal of Behavioral Decision Making* 29(5): 511–524. https://doi.org/10.1002/bdm.1897

National Safety Council. 2012. *Understanding the Distracted Brain: Why Driving While Using Hands-Free Cell Phones Is Risky Behavior.* https://www.nsc.org/getmedia/2ea8fe8b-d7b7-4194-8ea5-306d30a73972/cognitive-distraction-white-paper.lbndexpdf?srsltid=AfmBOopqV3H4PC8ZRjctw96nKkC8CLfAFbaJNK8sjXtB455mQxXaZeSU

Petty, Richard E. 1996. *Attitudes and Persuasion: Classic and Contemporary Approaches*. Routledge.

Pintrich, Paul R. 2000. "Multiple Goals, Multiple Pathways: The Role of Goal Orientation in Learning and Achievement." *Journal of Educational Psychology* 92(3): 544–555.

Ramey, Craig, Joseph Sparling, and Sharon Ramey. 2012. *Abecedarian: The Ideas, the Approach, and the Findings*. Sociometrics.

Redelmeier, Donald A., and Daniel Kahneman. 1996. "Patients' Memories of Painful Medical Treatments: Real-Time and Retrospective Evaluations of Two Minimally Invasive Procedures." *Pain* 66(1): 3–8. https://doi.org/10.1016/0304-3959(96)02994-6

Ryan, Richard M., and Edward L. Deci. 2000. "Self-Determination Theory and the Facilitation of Intrinsic Motivation, Social Development, and Well-being." *American Psychologist* 55(1): 68–78. https://psycnet.apa.org/doi/10.1037/0003-066X.55.1.68

Sanderson, Brandon. 2017. *Oathbringer*. Tor.

Shteynberg, Garriy, and Adam D. Galinsky. 2011. "Implicit Coordination: Sharing Goals with Similar Others Intensifies Goal Pursuit." *Journal of Experimental Social Psychology* 47: 1291–1294. https://doi:10.1016/j.jesp.2011.04.012

Singh, Rajesh. 2016. "The Impact of Intrinsic and Extrinsic Motivators on Employee Engagement in Information Organizations." *Journal of Education for Library and Information Science* 57(2): 197–206.

Skinner, B. F. 1938. *The Behavior of Organism*. Appleton-Century.

Skinner, B. F. 1987. "Whatever Happened to Psychology as the Science of Behavior?" *American Psychologist* 42(8): 780–786. https://psycnet.apa.org/doi/10.1037/0003-066X.42.8.780

Spence, J. David, Korbua Srichaikul, and David J. A. Jenkins. 2021. "Cardiovascular Harm from Egg Yolk and Meat: More Than Just Cholesterol and Saturated Fat." *Journal of the American Heart Association* 10(7). https://doi.org/10.1161/JAHA.120.017066

Thaler, Richard H., and Cass R. Sunstein. 2008. *Nudge: Improving Decisions About Health, Wealth, and Happiness.* Penguin.

Thibaut, John W., and Harold H. Kelley. 1959. *The Social Psychology of Groups*. Transaction Publishers.

Walesh, Stuart G. 2017. *Introduction to Creativity and Innovation for Engineers.* Pearson Education.

Willingham, Daniel T. 2021. *Why Don't Students Like School?* 2nd edition. Jossey Bass.

INDEX

C